For The Love Of A Child

Mary Ann Kinsey

Moonshine Press • Franklin, North Carolina

Published by:
Moonshine Press
162 Riverwood Drive
Franklin, NC 28734

www.moonshinepressnc.com

International Standard Book Number : 978-1720438731

Acknowledgements

I want to thank my husband, Jim, for his unwavering support and encouragement. He has been my everything for sixty-three years. My daughter Karyl and son Jimmy, have backed me every step of the way.

I also want to thank my niece, Jane Joyner Hampton, for sharing her research on the genealogy of the Hampton family.

A Special thanks to Deanna Lawrence for introducing me to the Writing Club. Without my Writing Club members, who were instrumental in encouraging and supporting me, this book might not have ever been completed. Thanks to each of you!

Thanks to my editor, Pamela Keyser and to Henry Fichner for the beautiful cover design.

Prologue

I was the youngest of nine children and grew up without either parent due to daddy's accident and mother's cancer, but my siblings and close relatives nurtured me.

God knew, before I was born, how my life would develop and grow. He does not make mistakes. He chose the right family for me. My teenage sister was my guardian and mentor. Mother's christian values and influence lived on through her.

At a young age, I committed my life to God's son, Jesus. I didn't understand theology, but I did understand God's love for me.

My desire, today, is still to please him with my life. He has blessed me and given me opportunities that I never could have experienced without Him.

Before I formed you in the womb, I knew you,
Before you were born, I set you apart, "says
The Lord
Jeremiah 1:5

Introduction

I had not even entered this world before my father was taken from me. But it was the mission of my six siblings to make sure that I had a place in our family. My mother was seven months pregnant with me at the time of my father's death. Concerned about my future life, she considered the Hephzibah Orphanage so that I, at least, could have a secure future, but my sisters and brothers saw things very differently. They had a love strong enough to shelter me and a determination to hold our family together. This same love bonded us five years later when the Lord took my mother away from us, too.

My sibling's ages ranged from eleven to twenty-one; many turns and twists would characterize my life as I headed toward an unsure future. However, another constant came into my life in those early years and gave me joy and eventually love, my future husband to whom I've been married 63 years. We met in the church we both attended when we were both eight years old.

God had a plan for me, even then - and for us! Though I don't see my story as remarkable, so many of those who know me think it is one worth telling. I must admit that my journey to becoming a teacher, a mother, and a wife has followed an unusual course. It was a journey that allowed me to grow a unique set of gifts that would serve me well in this life that has been characterized by love for and from colleagues, siblings, friends, and my children and husband.

In my story, as in so many, the way to break through boundaries, grow, learn from life lessons, share the joy in triumphs that comes from working with others, developing lifetime bonds, and having faith in a God that supports you when most needed.

During this 84th year in my life, I look back at the changes of a century: the impossible obstacles my siblings helped me to traverse, the path that led me to teaching, to acting, to lifelong friendships, to nurturing different generations of my own family, to holding the hand of a husband who built me my own Ferris wheel and a tree house where I could begin writing this book at the age of 82.

Life is a miracle, a blessing, God-given, and no moment of it should be wasted. I hope you will enjoy my story.

Chapter One

Daddy

My daddy died before I was born. He never got to hold me or see the deep blue of my eyes. I never got to sit on his lap and have him read me a story, nor run into his arms as he came through the door. He didn't see me graduate or walk me down the aisle at my wedding. I would have to hold him in my heart and know him from the stories told by my family, but his short life did leave me a legacy of love. The one he chose to be his wife, my mother, Bessie Mae Tyler told me he was a person of character. She married Charles Basil Hampton on January 1, 1916.

On April 24, 1933, the day my daddy died, started as a beautiful spring day. Daddy left for work early that morning, where he worked as a mechanic for the railroad. Mother started her day, as she did every day, by reading her well-worn Bible. Several passages underlined with pencil caught her attention. One verse found in I Thessalonians 5:18 reads, "Give thanks in all circumstances, for this is God's will for you." That would be a verse she would never forget.

The rest of the day was ordinary. As evening approached, the children, ranging from six to sixteen were busy getting homework and their clothes ready for school the next day. Betty, the youngest, was tucked in early. Daddy was supposed to come home late that evening. The children were all in bed when a knock at the door broke the silence.

Charles Basil Hampton and
Bessie Mae Tyler Hampton

Mother, seven months pregnant, with me, answered the knock. Turning on the porch light, she saw the policeman standing there in the shadows. With her heart pounding, she knew it was not good news. When the policeman in a very serious voice asked if Charles Hampton was her husband, she nodded her head as she opened the screen door and invited him inside. Standing in the long hallway, he told her that daddy had been in an accident and had not survived. Stunned by the news, she stood frozen in silence. Seeing her falter, the officer helped her sit down in a nearby chair. Then in the steadiest voice she could find, she called the older children, but they were already coming from their rooms somber and in disbelief. Sobs were muffled by faces buried in each other's arms.

The officer asked if he could notify anyone? Was there anyone who could come over to be with her and the children? Mother asked him to please contact Charlie's parents Reverend Preston Brooks Hampton and her sister, Mary Battle. No, she didn't want to disturb anyone at this hour, but she would send one of the boys, when it got light, to ask her friend to come over. Mother found something to write on in the desk drawer and wrote the addresses for Grandpa Hampton and Aunt Mary. With trembling hands, she gave the paper to the policeman. He walked slowly down the steps and to his patrol car.

Fear and disbelief filled the children's cries. Clinging to mother and following her into the living room, they had questions of why and how? What will we do? Mother held them close and reassured them with words that were difficult for even her to understand. She searched for the right words that she knew they needed, but with her heartache and scattered thoughts, words were difficult to express.

My daddy and three other workers hired a taxi to take them home that fateful night. On the drive home, the taxi driver did not see the speeding train approaching around a curve and drove into its path. Everyone in the taxi died that night. It was a tragic accident that claimed daddy's life. It was a tragedy talked about for days and especially about the young expectant mother of six left widowed, and expecting another child soon. According to the article in The Macon Telegraph, the bodies of the four men lay in Hart's Mortuary as hundreds of people passed through the building to view them. Crowds estimated at thousands visited the scene of the accident.

As news spread, people began bringing food and offering their heart-felt condolences. My sisters, Loyce and Virginia graciously accepted the many varieties of food items that friends brought when they came to express their sympathy. Mother thanked each one for their generosity and for thinking of them. After everyone was gone, her thoughts went back to the scripture she had read earlier that morning, "Give thanks in all circumstances." Breathing a prayer, she said, "Lord if that is what you want I will need your help."

Hart's Mortuary, in Macon, was in charge of daddy's funeral arrangements. The chapel filled with family and friends. My oldest brother, Charles, sat next to mother, keeping a close eye on her due to her frail condition. Grandpa Hampton asked a close friend of the family and pastor to be in charge of the service. Burial was at Riverside Cemetery in Macon, next to the two tiny graves of Helen, and Billy, my bother, and sister who had died as babies.

Virginia's birthday was in two days. It was hard enough to be excited about your birthday when your daddy had just died, but now, his funeral was on that same day. The worst thing she would have to do was say goodbye to daddy, for the last time, on her birthday. Her life changed forever. Hers seemed more personal, even though, all of them had their lives changed forever. Every year on April 24 it would be a reminder of the last time she saw daddy.

Virginia, nine, wondered if mother would bake her birthday cake like she always did for each one on their birthday. She was hoping to get the dime that mother put in it. Mother made sure the birthday child got the slice of cake that had the ten cents in it. Mother had a lot on her mind, but she would not forget a birthday. Virginia got her cake, but it was a day late.

The older children carried some of the burdens in their teenage hearts. They were old enough to see how this had affected mother. Being concerned about her physical condition, they tried to make things easier around the house. Even when mother smiled, they could see the sadness in her demeanor.

Loyce, thirteen, was a natural in the kitchen and took on the responsibility of preparing their meals. Virginia, helped by washing the dishes. She didn't like doing dishes, but she knew everybody had to help. Even though Betty was only six, she tried to help by picking up her toys.

The boys picked vegetables from the garden and loaded them in my fifteen-year-old brother, P.B.'s little red wagon. They pulled the red-cart through the neighborhood selling to anyone who needed fresh vegetables. Sometimes they brought twenty-five cents home to mother. On a good day, they might get fifty-cents. Every penny was important during the depression.

Time came and went, day after day, week after week. Sometimes time stood still, other times it raced by, but each one had adjusted into a routine for moving forward with their lives. Mother kept herself busy with the sewing that she loved and was looking forward to the soon to be new baby. She had always made the children's clothes, including the boy's shirts. Needing to make a living, she took in sewing for other families. She was also a barber, though she never had a barber's chair. Her Barber's License issued by the City of Macon, State of Georgia was placed in a window for her clients to see. She charged fifteen cents per haircut whether for a child or an adult. Sometimes she would advertise on Saturdays "Hair Cuts, today, ten cents." No one was turned away even if they could not pay the ten cents that she charged.

It was eventually settled that the Central of Georgia Railroad was at fault in daddy's death, due to the excessive speed of the train. Sometime later, the railroad offered his sons jobs. That was a welcomed, unexpected opportunity and the boys worked hard. Charles worked there as a teen doing laborer jobs and advanced gradually. Finally, as an adult, he became an engineer and worked there until his retirement in 1972.

Harold married at seventeen and was married over sixty years to his wife, Ruth. He was a building contractor, building Bel Arbor Nursing Home, in Macon, that was family owned. Later, he followed his calling into the ministry. He pastored a Methodist church and then was pastor to the children at The Hephzibah Children's Home, in Macon, that was founded by our Great Aunt Bettie Tyler in 1900. When the Hephzibah home was ready to expand, they asked Harold to oversee the building project. He accepted the opportunity and continued to pastor churches in Macon until 1967.

Chapter Two
My Birth

Everyone was trying to move forward, and with mother's positive attitude, the good in their lives was reinforced even though there had been a sad change in the family in the last two months. Mother had been making baby gowns and kimonos, for me, with dainty lace and tiny buttons down the front. Delicate blankets with pink ribbon were still on the chest near the Singer, peddle sewing machine when mother announced it was time for her to go to the hospital for the arrival of the baby they had waited for so long. Mother had had all her children at home before now. I was going to be her first baby born in a hospital. Everyone was excited and anxious.

Grandmother was there when she left. I was born, Mary Annette Hampton on June 21, 1933. After a week in the hospital, it was time for mother to go home with me. Loyce was there to ride with her. While holding me on the way to the house, she asked mother if they could shorten my name from Mary Annette to just Mary Ann. Mother told her that my legal name was Mary Annette, but it was okay to call me Mary Ann. From that day, I have been Mary Ann. Mother was weak and tired from the ride home, so she took a short rest while Loyce took care of me.

Loyce became my second mother. She bathed and dressed me every day in the dainty little handmade gowns that mother had made for me. Often, she would walk me around the block in the baby carriage to show me off to the neighbors. Within a few months, I had grown into a little blue-eyed, happy, baby with blonde curls and a dimple in my chin just like my big brother, Charles.

Me at 16 Months Old

By the time I was a year old, I was walking in white high-top shoes that were polished every day with white shoestrings removed and washed before being laced in the shoes to be worn again. Mother always said she wanted sweet smelling, clean babies. Loyce learned, from mother, how to take care of me.

When I was less than two years old, another tragedy struck! Mother, at the suggestion and persistence of her doctor, went into the hospital for a series of tests. The results of the tests on my mother revealed she had ovarian cancer. How could she face another devastating report, more devastating than daddy's death? What would happen to the children? Again, there was that scripture "Be thankful in all circumstances."

Thinking of the children first, she had to be strong, and she would depend on her faith to sustain her, but how could she tell the children? When she came home, from the doctor's office, the older children asked her what the doctor said. Trying to minimize it, she told them there were some treatments she would need to have, and the treatments could cure the disease.

Radiation was a new treatment for cancer in the 1930's. Thankfully, mother was one of the first recipients of radiation in Macon. However, the doctors were not hopeful. Mother had to accept the fact that she could die. How could she leave teenagers with the responsibility and burden of raising me? Of course, there was the Hephzibah Orphanage in Macon that our Great Aunt Bettie Tyler had founded. Mother and grandmother Tyler had both worked there as housemothers at one time. The question was heavy on her heart every day. As much as she loved the Hephzibah, she knew there was always the possibility that of one or more of the children would be adopted and separated. She and daddy had themselves adopted one of the children who lived with them for several years until one day his dad showed up and took him away.

Praying that the radiation would kill the cancer, she still had to consider the future of her children. Psalm34:18 "The Lord is close to the brokenhearted and helps those who are crushed in spirit" is a scripture that would give her hope. Mother still had some decisions to make. It was on her mind every waking moment.

She was getting weaker each day, and it was becoming more visible in her physical appearance. She was admitted to Macon General Hospital again to continue the radiation treatments, even though it was evident that the cancer was continuing to spread. Loyce visited her every day after school, often helping the nurses with mother's general care. Loyce cherished every day with her. Mother was her mentor and her rock. Virginia and Betty visited her and on occasion brought me along. I had no way of knowing the gravity of the situation. The nurses and the staff allowed us to visit as they recognized the seriousness and urgency for mother to see us as it was for us to see her. Grandmother, again, moved in with us as she always did when she was needed. She and Aunt Mary were both concerned about our future.

Mother still believed that God could perform a miracle and heal her. She never gave up. One-day God took her to death's door, but then she began to rally. The nurses couldn't believe the improvement that they were seeing. She told the head nurse that the Lord had healed her, and she felt well enough to go home and would like for her to call a cab for her. Knowing that mother had the right to make that decision and after talking with the doctor, she called a cab as mother had requested.

When mother arrived home, she got out of the cab, walked up a steep set of concrete steps to the front porch where grandmother was sitting. Grandmother was in a state of disbelief and shock. She tried to usher mother to bed, but she insisted on sitting on the porch for a while and told her how the Lord had healed her. It was an amazing story.

Each day mother gained more strength, and the children began to relax a little. It was such a relief to see her more like herself. The children became children again without some of the burdens they had been carrying. It was a wonderful, happy time without the stress of mother being sick. She was well for a year, and I was about two and a half before the cancer returned. She was thankful for the extra year that God gave her to prepare the children for their life ahead. She still had to make the most difficult decision of her life. She knew the children would not be able to, nor should they have to, make such a serious decision.

She thought about a couple, Kenneth and Ollie Hall, that she had met, who had no children with no hope of having any. She had talked to them before about how much they wanted a child. They knew that mother was very sick and when they saw me, they asked if there was a possibility that she would let them adopt me. At that time, she couldn't make that decision. Now, however, she realized she needed to prepare herself and the children for the inevitable.

She invited them over to talk again about the possibility of them adopting me. After talking to them, at length, she felt the right thing to do was to let them adopt me.

Without telling the children of her decision, she made arrangements, with them, for me to go with them, the next week, to live in Birmingham, Alabama. My siblings thought it was for a visit and thought it would give mother some relief and take away some of the stress from her, temporarily, since she was beginning to show signs of fatigue. The day that the Halls came for me, my clothes were packed, and all of my siblings came to say goodbye. However, when I was not home for my birthday, they started questioning mother about why I was not home. It was then that mother had to explain to them what she had done and why she had done it. She told them that she had done it out of love and consideration for them and hoped they would understand. She had to reveal to them that she knew that it was possible that she might not live long enough to raise me and didn't want to leave them with that responsibility since I was only three-years-old, and it would be many years before

I would be able to take care of myself. I am sure they didn't realize the pain she suffered, those months while making that decision.

They had never heard mother say that she might die. They had not wanted to consider that and were devastated at the thought and, now, I was gone. It was the worse day they had had in recent weeks. They felt their world was caving in, but mother talked to them about

Me at 3 Years Old their life if those things did happen and what

was involved in raising a three-year-old twenty-four hours a day for years. Mother told them it could restrict and probably would restrict their lives. They insisted that they could make it work and, in fact, were determined to make it work. My older brother, who was now the father figure, agreed that they wanted me and needed me. He said I was the only sunshine in their lives some days. They convinced mother that she had worried needlessly.

Mother listened to their love for me and how they were willing to sacrifice their own lives to take care of me. The Bible verse came to mind again, "Be thankful in all circumstances". She was thankful that her children who cared enough for each other to take a little child and be committed to her for life. The devastating decision that she had made, possibly, could have been resolved without the anguish that she had experienced if she had just talked to my siblings about it first.

Mother thought about the Halls and how this would affect them. She knew they would be deeply hurt and wasn't sure how they would handle this. Since we had no phone, there was no good way for her to apologize to them or tell them how horrible she felt about her decision without discussing this with the children. She was in no condition to travel in order to talk to them herself, so she wrote a

My Birthday At The Halls

letter to try to express her regrets and sorrow for the situation. She expressed her desire to keep in touch with them so that they might see me.

Charles, twenty-one, was now our provider and had a job that he couldn't afford to jeopardize by taking time off. It was decided that Harold, nineteen, was the only one that could make the trip to Birmingham to talk to the Halls and, hopefully, bring me home. He checked the train schedule and was able to get a ticket that day. It was late at night when he arrived in Birmingham, but he took a cab to the Halls home. They must have been surprised to see him at that hour, but they were gracious and talked to him. When he told them the reason for his unexpected visit, they were quiet and stunned. After discussing what was best for me and how I had become a part of them, they explained how well I had adjusted to my new environment. Harold gave them the letter that mother had written to them. As they read the letter, he saw tears stream down their faces. They told Harold, through tears, that I was happy, but they realized how this had changed his family, too. He expressed how each one in the family felt about me and that they didn't know that mother had planned to let them adopt me. Both the Halls and Harold were crying, each understanding the pain the other was feeling. After a while, taking time to compose themselves, they led him into the room where I was asleep. Waking me up, Ollie and Kenneth told me that Harold was here and gave me a big hug and kiss with wet cheeks and handed me over to Harold without incident. It was a long night of agony for both families. Of course, I was happy to see him and went with him willingly. Riding on the train, I soon fell asleep while Harold had to relive the past few hours in his mind and heart. With a more mature understanding than he had before he arrived at the Halls, he felt an overwhelming love for them and tears began to well up in his eyes as he looked at me sleeping and realizing the emptiness and heartache of losing me that the Halls had accepted so selfless and kind. I arrived home with Harold to many hugs and kisses. I never understood what had just happened. I simply knew I was loved. Everyone agreed that our home was complete again, but never minimized what Kenneth and Ollie Hall did for us.

We had mother two more years. Even though some things were normal, mother was still sick, and I had the Whooping Cough. The cough took my breath away. I remember how my brothers threw me up in the air to help me catch my breath. That went on all day and sometimes all night. Without their attention to my coughing, I might not have survived. Mother's health was declining every day. The family knew that she could not live much longer.

The day she died, she was at home. Family members came over for emotional support more than anything else, as there was nothing anyone could do. Some sat in the long wide hallway just outside her room allowing her children, her mother and sister have those last minutes with her. One of daddy's nieces held me until it was evident she would be gone quickly. With the children surrounding her bed, she sat partway up and said, "I see a light. It is Jesus". Those were her last words. I was quickly taken in her room with the other children to see her for the last time. I was five years old when she died at the young age of 43 on August 1, 1938.

Front: Betty, me
Back: Loyce, Jenny

Hart's Mortuary handled her funeral arrangements just as they had done for daddy. The funeral chapel was filled with familiar and unfamiliar faces on that hot summer day. My sisters remembered the dresses they were wearing that day, and I remember them describing my dress in detail. It was probably one that mother had made for me. My brother held me up to her satin lined casket so that I could see her and tell her goodbye. I remember kissing her on the forehead. I was surprised at how cold she was, not warm like the mother I knew. Maybe that was when the stark reality of death became real to me. I never forgot that feeling, though I never mentioned it to my siblings or anyone else. I never wanted to hurt anyone or make them feel bad. If I said anything about that to them, they might feel bad and think they had done something wrong in letting me touch her. Everything they did for me was out of love.

She was buried at Riverside Cemetery in Macon, Georgia next to daddy and the two children they lost as infants. I have been able to visit and put flowers on their graves over the years. I never leave with sadness, but thankful for the time I knew her.

Kenneth and Ollie Hall were wonderful people. We kept in touch with them for years. Mother had been instrumental in helping them adopt a beautiful baby boy who was slightly mentally challenged. They loved him dearly and were awesome parents to him. When I was in elementary school, I spent time with them in the summers. I treated their little boy, Jerry, like he was my brother. Jerry and I grew up in different states. I lost contact and didn't see them for several years. The last time I saw Ollie and Jerry, I was married. I took my daughter, Karyl, to see them when she was a year old and found out Kenneth had died several months earlier. I have very happy memories of them.

Chapter Three

Siblings

I owe who I am today to the love and guidance my brothers and sisters gave me. Each one gave me something that wove a positive thread into the fabric of my life.

Charles Basil Hampton
Charles

Charles, the oldest, became the patriarch in the family when our father died. He was an engineer for the Central of Georgia Railroad. He took care of us in every way. He put us first for years. At forty years old he finally met and married a wonderful lady. Cleo was perfect for him. She fit into our family, loving us and we could only return that kind of love with love for her. Charles was a very unselfish person.

He not only provided us with a home, but he spent time with us and made Christmas like a wonderland of gifts for each of us. He had a happy, positive attitude about life. He never let us know if there was a problem. He was our hero. When Charles died, Hart's Mortuary, in Macon, Georgia handled his service, and he is buried in Riverside Cemetery, Macon, Georgia.

Virginia Faith Hampton
(Jenny)

When Loyce married and moved to Florida with her husband, I went with them. Jenny and Betty went to live with Aunt Mary and Uncle Warren and grandmother. After Grandmother died they left the country and moved to Valdosta where Uncle Warren was still working for the Southern Railroad.

Jenny was shy and studious. She was the first one to graduate from high school in our family. Soon after graduating from Valdosta High School, she applied for a job at the Pentagon in Arlington Virginia. She got the job, left home at nineteen to work as a secretary for a general at the Pentagon. She admits that she was terrified when she left home. Aunt Mary had to push her, but she knew Jenny needed the job and she also knew she needed to gain some confidence. Jenny often said that was the best thing Aunt Mary could have ever done for her. She was forced to move out of her comfort zone. She blossomed into a confident and successful person.

While living in Arlington, with her roommate, Jean Hartz, she met Jean's brother, Sam, and eventually married him and moved to Weatherly, Pennsylvania. After the birth of two girls, Joycelyn and Gail, they moved to Warner Robins, Georgia where they both worked at Robins Air Force Base. Jenny worked for several Generals before she became a Computer Programmer. Both she and Sam retired from Robbins Air Force Base in Warner Robins, Georgia.

Jenny and I were very close as adults. We shared many interests and tastes. We enjoyed traveling together and eating out. We reminisced about how thinking had changed so much over time. Since we were depression children, our Grandmother (Chattie) Tyler wanted us to be on our best behavior particularly when we ate at some one's home. She thought if we cleaned our plate people would think we didn't have enough to eat at home. So, she would say, just leave a bite of food on your plate for good manners.

That was a standing joke with Jenny and me. When we finished eating, one of us would usually say, "I'm leaving this last bite for Chattie." We never called her Chattie in her presence. We loved her, and she had a great influence on our lives.

I lost Jenny, at eighty-nine years of age on November 1, 2013, just thirteen days after Loyce died at ninety-three years of age on October 19, 2013. I lost my two best friends that year. That left me the last living sibling.

Preston Brooks Hampton
P. B.

P. B. was named after Grandpa, Preston Brooks Hampton. He was only fifteen years old when mother died. That was an awkward

P.B., 1944

age for a boy. Not knowing how to handle life, he married young, and it did not work out.

He went into the service during World War II at a young age. We wrote letters and sent packages to him while he was stationed in South Africa. While in Italy, he sent me a beautiful white china demitasse tea set with delicate pink roses on each of the twelve cups and saucers.

The teapot and creamer and sugar bowl had the same design. I was ten when it arrived in the mail. I loved playing with it as it reminded me of him. It is displayed in my china cabinet today.

While in the military he received the Purple Heart for bravery, but I never heard him say what he had done to receive such an honor.

I treasure it today, and I remember the day he came home from the war like it was yesterday. I was in fifth grade, and my grandmother sent our maid to the school to tell me they had just heard that he would be home that day. I was excused to leave class and go home to meet him when he arrived. This was a special day for me. I was so excited; I remember actually trembling as I walked home. It was a special day when anyone came home from service. When he returned from the war, he was not the same person. He probably had PTSD (Post Traumatic Syndrome Disorder), but that was not recognized at that time. Planes flying overhead would cause him to duck his head, thinking it was an enemy plane. He died in a hospital in Atlanta, Georgia with a damaged heart at the age of thirty-four. Hart's Mortuary handled his funeral, and he is buried in Riverside Cemetery near daddy, mother and Helen and Betty's twin, Billy

Betty Lou Hampton
Betty

As a young child, Betty was the one who thought up things to do that would have been better forgotten. She was not a malicious child; she just had too much energy to waste.

One afternoon, she was playing outside when grandma announced that she was going to the barn to milk the cow and told her not to get on top of the barn while she was milking. Well, that sounded like an invitation to Betty, so she got on the barn and danced. Of course, the cow kicked and spilled the milk. She was in trouble again!

She was outgoing with a happy-go-lucky attitude and had lots of friends. She was a cheerleader in high school and was always wanting to drive the family car. One day the car was parked out front of the house, so she and her cheerleader friends decided they might take it to their meeting.

Betty got the key and tried the ignition several times, and when it didn't start, they thought pushing it might work. They moved it over and over little by little trying to start it until they had pushed it all the way around the block before giving up.

When Uncle Warren came home, Betty told him there was something wrong with the car because it wouldn't start. He smiled and said he thought she might try that, so he took the battery out. Uncle Warren was always funny, but she didn't think he was funny that day. At least she didn't get in trouble. I guess he thought she had had enough difficulty for one day.

Betty married and had two daughters, Donna Carlos and Karen Mitchell. Betty had a full life, but contracted Parkinson's Disease. She died in 2005 and is buried in Athens, Georgia.

William Harold Hampton
Harold

Harold fell in love, as a teenager, to his future wife, Ruth Hamby when he was seventeen and Ruth was fifteen. They begged mother to sign for them to get married. Of course, the answer from mother was no. After months of nagging and after mother sat them down and talked to them about marriage and the odds of teenagers making it work long term were doubtful or slim, she finally gave her consent.

They married when he was seventeen, and she was fifteen. He became a successful businessman, minister, and a great father to two children, Charles and Brenda. Harold and Ruth established their own home from the beginning and never lived with us. When their first child, a son, was born they named him after our older brother, Charles. Therefore, he was dubbed Baby Charles. That name followed him into adulthood, to his embarrassment and dismay.

Harold and Ruth were married over sixty years until his death. He was absolutely in love with her from day one. He adored her and spoiled her completely. They are both buried in Monroe County, Georgia.

Me, Betty, Jenny, Loyce, Harold, Charles

Chapter Four

Sister's Gift

Loyce Evelyn Hampton

Loyce

Now that we were settled in the upstairs apartment in Macon everyone felt like a family again. It is surprising how everyone adjusted to the change in our family and how they cooperated with each other. Life was good because of my older siblings. Each one of them contributed to the sense of security that I have today.

Loyce, 1942

At seventeen, the responsibility of home and younger sisters was thrust upon Loyce's sensitive yet, strong shoulders. Being quiet and timid she was forced to reach out for a boldness and a new strength, a strength that would sustain her in her time of grief. The four years of agonizing over the inevitable demise of mother had not prepared her for the shock when it came as this was the second time of unbearable grief. Our father had been taken away suddenly in a car accident just five years prior to today.

Mother had been a close and valued friend. One who trusted her to make decisions about the home. One who guided and inspired her. One who taught her homemaking skills that she now would need on a daily basis.

The strength of her character was exhibited as she took care of

28

three younger sisters and kept our home going as smoothly as when mother had been there. Not only did she take care of the household duties that most teenagers resist, but she was a gifted seamstress. The clothes that she made for us were no small feat. Each stitch was carefully intertwined with love. Her specialties included tucks, pleats, appliques, embroidery, smocking and hand-sewn lace. She took pride in our appearance making sure that our hair was clean, curled, and brushed and our hair ribbons and socks matched our dresses that she had sewn, and many without the use of a pattern.

She attended P.T.A. for each of us and participated in all school functions. Now, she admits she felt awkward at such functions being the youngest "mother" there. We never knew, nor could we have understood at that time, what her sacrifice was. When she was making crepe paper dresses for us to dance around the Maypole and entering my eleven-year-old sister in the Little Miss Macon Contest, we were like all other children whose mothers did those kinds of things. She kept our lives as normal as possible creating a bond between us and keeping us a family.

As a result of having a mother who taught and instilled christian values, Loyce lived the same kind of life as an example for us. Honesty was expected even in small situations at home and school. It was these values that showed me the importance of having a good character. Prayer and Bible reading before retiring for the night and before every meal taught us the value of worship and about Jesus' love for us.

Recognizing her need to spend time with other young people her age, our twenty-one-year-old brother, Charles, who also put his life on hold to support us financially, encouraged her to attend a youth retreat with other church youth from Lakeland, Florida. The Lakeland youth group riding in an open-bed truck with high slat sides covered only with a tarpaulin spread over metal ribs above, to protect them from the elements, stopped to pick up the youth group in Macon, Georgia. Bouncing along, on hand-crafted wooden benches, singing and making new friends made this trip to Oakdale, Kentucky memorable.

Not only did this retreat prove to be a faith-strengthening experience, but it was coupled with Loyce meeting her future husband. This special young man traveled from Florida to Georgia on numerous occasions to visit her. Obviously, this was a serious relationship, but, again not wanting to upset the lives of the girls during the school year, a secret marriage was planned and ultimately carried out.

Noticing some subtle changes in Loyce's behavior, this caring brother became suspicious that she had gotten married and over her denials, he set out to confirm his suspicions. He, indeed, did find the marriage license and Certificate of Marriage locked away in her cedar chest. Curiosity could have killed the cat, but he was forgiven, and it was determined that she would go to Florida to live with her husband.

All family members were notified, and arrangements were made for the two older girls, Jenny and Betty to go live with our mother's sister, Aunt Mary, who had promised our mother, on her death bed, that she would take care of the children. She was a major part of our lives until her death at the age of ninety.

Loyce had total responsibility of me since my birth in 1933. Now, eight years old and the youngest of the girls, it was decided that I would go with her to Florida. Her husband welcomed me and again it was another one of God's plans to direct my path. Eventually, Loyce and her husband had three children, Glenda, Jenny and Wes, but I was always their child and the sister to their children.

Loyce

Loyce was always a thoughtful person, never putting herself first. When mother was sick, Loyce left school to assume responsibility for our family. She later returned to school and completed her education.

Loyce loved poetry and taught me to memorize my first poem for a church Christmas program when I was two years old. She never had the opportunity to act publicly, but she often performed for us at home. She didn't just recite poetry; she made it come alive. Little did she realize that she was "performing poetry." Today, Poetry Alive is being taught in schools and is considered a valued form of Oral Art.

The blessing of wisdom is found in Proverbs 3:6 which says, "I all thy ways acknowledge him, and he will direct thy paths". Without Loyce's wisdom, her love and her mature nurturing, my life could have taken a different

Loyce's 90th Birthday

path, but it is evident that her faithful service to Jesus both directed her path and mine.

31

Loyce died October 19 2013 at the age of 93.

Chapter Five

A Memorable Train Ride

First, sounds of crying, then screams shattered the peaceful, quiet of the passengers on the train ride from Macon, to Atlanta. Startled passengers craned their necks to see what the fuss was all about. "Who is that?" "What is happening?"

A five-year-old child, had locked herself in the ladies' restroom. That child was me, terrified when I couldn't open the door!

When the conductor came and un-locked the door, I grabbed Loyce, and she hugged me tight and wiped away my tears.

I was embarrassed as we walked back

Me at 5 years old

to our seats when I heard one lady say, "Poor little scared thing", I guess I didn't realize everyone had heard me, but I felt safe with Loyce, my second mother, now that mother was gone.

I was riding the train from Macon to Atlanta with my sister, Loyce. I wore one of the hand-sewn dresses that mother had made for me shortly before cancer took her from us. Loyce, always made sure that my outfit and socks matched, and that I had a ribbon in my blonde curls. I had on freshly polished white high-top shoes with snow white shoestrings. She continued what mother had always stressed; cleanliness was next to godliness.

At the beginning of the trip, I had walked down the aisle with confidence to our seats, but after the bathroom incident, I crawled onto my seat and sat quietly for the rest of the trip.

I rode on the Central of Georgia passenger train many times after that, but I never forgot that terrifying experience. I can say, "That was truly a Memorable Train Ride".

Chapter Six
Talbotton, Georgia

After mother's death, we tried to get settled in a different home that would help us adjust to our new situation. However, when we relocated, there were those who chose to frighten a house of teenagers, making it necessary to move again seeking a safe place.

After several of these intrusions, my brother, Charles, being concerned about our safety had Virginia, Betty and me move with Aunt Mary and Uncle Warren again. They had moved from Macon to the country in the small community of Junction City, Georgia just outside of Columbus with Grandmother Tyler moving with them. Uncle Warren worked for the Southern Railroad in Valdosta and came home on weekends. Charles and Loyce stayed in Macon to

Grandmother "Chattie" Tyler

look for a safer place for us to live.

When we arrived, by Greyhound, at the Greyhound Bus Stop at the Po Biddy Crossroads, Aunt Mary met us in her little green Chevrolet and drove us over dry, dusty roads back to Junction City. The population in 1940 couldn't have had many residents because the populous was only 179 in the year 2000.

We were excited to see Grandmother and our new home. It was a big white house with a swing on the end of the big front porch where we spent many hours swinging and singing. There were many varieties of flowers behind a white picket fence. Out back, there was a vegetable garden, lots of chickens from little bantam roosters to big red rock hens and two or three pigs in a pen away from the house. At this time, during the depression, one could see many homes surrounded by gardens and farm animals to provide food for their families.

To our surprise, our new house had no electricity nor plumbing. There was a well out back with a bucket tied with a rope to a log that was turned slowly, by a handle to allow the bucket to go down into the well. We could hear the bucket hit the water and when it was full, the handle had to be turned slowly to bring the bucket back up where the water was poured into a container that had to be carried into the kitchen. There was an outhouse out back near the chicken pen instead of a bathroom inside the house. This was all new to us since we were from the city, but it was also intriguing. We used oil lamps for light, which meant that when it got dark, we went to bed.

Aunt Mary

After a few months, Aunt Mary had the power company run electricity to the house from the nearest town of Talbotton. After watching the workmen put up power poles and run the electric lines to the house, we were anxious for it to be completed. Aunt Mary ordered light fixtures from Sears, but we had to wait for them to come in the mail. When they were finally installed, we were ecstatic. Now we could read after dark.

Grandmother tended the many varieties of flowers in the flower beds separated by walkways behind the white picket fence. She loved anything that she could plant. She was a prim and proper lady with silver gray hair that was always neatly put up into a bun on the back of her head. I can still see her sauntering along the paths of flowers admiring each bloom with her little lace-trimmed handkerchief in her hand.

We loved it when Uncle Warren came home on the weekends. He was funny and fun to be around. If we saw someone walking down that country road, we would wait and watch from a distance, to see if they stopped to scratch their back on a tree. If they did, we knew it was Uncle Warren. That was a habit of his, and we thought it was hilarious.

Uncle Warren

He loved to fish and would take us with him. We would get up early and get all the fishing poles and the can of worms that he had dug from under the rocks in the flower beds the day before. Then, we got in the car for the drive to the lake or fishing hole. He would stick five or six cane poles in the bank, so the line would drop into the water. Then he would walk around to see what the other fishermen were catching. Betty and I would follow him every step looking like a brood of ducklings, I'm sure. Later, when he came back to check on his poles, they were just like he left them - empty. We never caught any fish to take home. I think it was just a way for him to enjoy being outside. I'm sure Aunt Mary was not waiting on fish for dinner.

When we came home late and hungry, there was usually fresh, hot, juicy chicken that grandmother had killed, dressed and fried to perfection. The ginger bread that had warm white sauce poured over the top was mouthwatering.

After dinner, Uncle Warren was ready for a game of checkers. He would more or less, bribe us to play with him, because in the country unless he drove to a friend's house for a game of checkers, he needed a partner.

Another board game favorite of his was a game called Caroms. It was played on a big square wooden board with net-pockets on each corner. It was painted like a checkerboard making it a two-game board. The object of the game caroms was to thump, with your fingers, discs into the pockets. Thumping discs with your fingers, made them sore, so we seldom could win. When he saw we were going to quit, he would let us win a game to keep us playing for a while.

He was also a practical joker. One day he came home from a walk through the woods with a snapping turtle and put it on Aunt Mary while she was napping. Of course, he called us in to see her reaction. It was not as dramatic as he had hoped.

One afternoon, Aunt Mary took us three restless girls with her to visit her friends, Baker and Mattie Baldwin. While Aunt Mary and Miss Mattie (as we were taught to address her) were visiting on the big front porch, we went out back with Mr. Baker to see the animals. He loved children and let us do about anything as long as it was safe.

Betty never missed an opportunity to have fun. Today was no different. After watching the little goats for a while, she decided she wanted one of Mr. Baker's goats. Being six years older than me, she could get me involved in about anything. After chasing one of the goats trying to catch it, Mr. Baker told her if she could capture it

she could have it. That set Betty's determination in motion and with my help
we chased that little goat until he was
exhausted and let us catch him. Mr. Baker
was sitting on the split-rail fence enjoying
the fray.

Now, that we had him, how were we
going to get him to our house? I knew
Betty would know what to do. Yep, she
had the solution. We would put him in the

Me at seven years old

backseat of Aunt Mary's car. Pushing and pulling, he was finally
secure in the car. Mr. Baker watched with amusement and pleasure.

What a surprise when Aunt Mary got ready to leave and came
out to her car and saw a goat in the backseat baaing for help. Seeing
our delight and with the squealing from us, she actually drove home
with that goat baaing all the way. We put him in the field near the
house. The next morning, to our dismay, he was gone. We learned
later that Mr. Baker had taken him back home.

Fall was in the air, and we were thinking about school. Aunt
Mary was buying us clothes and classroom supplies. The school was
in Talbotton, eighteen miles from our house. I was going to finish
second grade in the same building as Virginia and Betty. This school
taught grades one through eleven. When the students completed the
eleventh grade, they received their diploma. I was going to ride a big
yellow school bus. It was exciting! I was used to walking to school
in Macon. One of the good things about riding the school bus was,
the bus driver stopped every afternoon at Hester's Country Store
and let us go in and buy a snack for the last part of our ride home.

The first year that we were there, Aunt Mary had to drive us about five miles to meet the school bus over dry, dusty, red clay roads twice a day. They were rough and bumpy when dry, but after a good rain, the car would slide back and forth across the road. After a while, she decided it would be easier to pay the school district to have the bus driver pick us up at our driveway.

By the end of the summer, Charles and Loyce had found an upstairs apartment in a two-story house, in Macon. We girls, moved back home to live as a family again. Having a family living down-stairs, gave everyone a more secure feeling.

Whittle Grammar School backed up to our yard, and there was a brick wall that was eight feet high from our backyard, but it was only about a foot high on the school grounds. Walking the wall from the schoolyard, I didn't realize how high it was down to my yard. Making a wrong step, I slipped and fell the entire eight feet down into my backyard. After a trip to the hospital, it was determined that I was not hurt seriously. After a few days of rest, I was fine and never walked the wall again.

Chapter Seven

Toys and Activities in 1930's and 1940's

Growing up in the '30's and '40's, I have good memories of many outside activities. When I was four or five years old, my older sisters took me on walks through the woods, behind our house, to pick wild flowers and marvel at the birds flitting from tree to tree or the rabbits darting about or the chickadees chirping. Seeing a patch of green moss growing on the ground, I would tell them about the fairies that lived there. There was a magical fairy dance for me.

One toy that I had at that age was a Little Orphan Annie electric stove. Jenny would help me bake little tiny cupcakes in the oven. Paper dolls were popular when I was a little older. They had beautiful clothes and I could change their clothes and pretend for them to be anyone I wanted them to be.

Every little girl had at least one baby doll. My sister, Loyce, made doll clothes for my dolls. One Christmas, she made a doll cedar chest full of handmade clothes for them. I still have the chest and a doll high chair that I got that same Christmas.

Me at eight years old

The bicycle that I got when I was eight was a shiny blue with a black leather seat and handlebar grips. Loyce taught me how to ride by running along with me and finally let me go by myself. I'm sure it took many times for me to learn how to balance as training wheels had not yet been invented. It was the only bicycle that I ever owned. I rode it for years, probably, because I had to put it on the porch at night and take care of it. Riding that bike, was the thing that I enjoyed the most.

Being an outside girl, my skates were another one of my favorite outdoor activities. Shoes with soles were required as skates had clamps that had to be tightened onto our shoe soles with a key that you wore on a string around your neck. Sometimes, the clamps would come off and you had to stop and take your key and tighten them again. Another good thing about them was that they could be lengthened to fit our shoes as we grew. My brother-in-law was a great skater and we would often go roller skating at the Orlando coliseum on Saturday nights.

In elementary school, we used to play "Jack Stones" that began by gently throwing small stones (or rocks) onto the sidewalk in front of where you were sitting. Then, the object was to toss a small ball up in the air and quickly pick up some of the stones and catch the ball on the first bounce. The game is played the same way today, but instead of stones (or rocks), little plastic or metal objects are used.

I remember, one time, sweeping out our chicken house to use for a playhouse. It didn't last long because you can sweep it clean, but it is still dusty, and you can't make it smell like orange blossoms. The chickens were happy to move back in.

I loved acrobatics, though I never had a lesson. I guess you could say I was self-taught through trial and error. I could turn flips on the lawn without using my hands. I would get a running start and propel my body up in the air and at the same time, tuck my head and flip over landing on my feet.

Another trick I tried was to climb a tree upside down, but that did not go well. I tried standing on my hands and pushing my feet against the tree. When I picked my hands up to grab the tree trunk, of course, my head hit the ground. I got up with my head favoring one side. Going home holding my head with my hand to keep it from falling off, at least it felt like it might. My sister called a chiropractor friend, who came, to the house and put me back together. It sounds dumb, I know, but I was smart enough not to try it again.

Uncle Warren made me wooden stilts that were made with two six-foot-tall square poles with a block of wood attached to each pole about two feet from the bottom of the pole. I had to grab the poles, holding them under my arms while I stepped on each block. I had to stand on the blocks and balance before I started walking. I walked for hours, but when I complained that my arches hurt, because I had no arches, Aunt Mary would let the stilts disappear. After time passed, I would beg for another pair. Uncle Warren would make them, and the same thing occurred - walk - complain with pain in my arches again - lose stilts.

He also made me jumping boards. He used a wide plank ten or twelve inches wide and about ten feet long. The long board was placed over a short log with the board even on both ends. Then, two people could step on the board, one on each end, and jump sending each other up and down, much like a see saw.

Chapter Eight

Hephzibah Orphanage

A game of kickball after school was interrupted by shouts of "Smoke," "Smoke," coming from someone near the house. The house was the Hephzibah Orphanage. Children were running in all directions calling Miss Bettie! Miss Bettie! As Miss Bettie came around the house, flames were already shooting out of the kitchen windows. The frame structure was being eaten by the angry blaze.

The children! Where are the children? Mollie, get the children! Check the girls' rooms! Get out! It's going fast!

With sirens screaming, the fire truck turned into the driveway. Firemen ran toward the raging fire, dragging their long water hose over the rocky, uneven ground. Another fire truck arrived, the flames were licking toward the sky above the tree line. After an hour of battling the blaze, and exhausting their water supply, the firemen watched helplessly, along with the crowd that had gathered, as the home to 75 - 100 orphans lay in ashes.

Great-Aunt Bettie Tyler, founder of Hephzibah Orphanage

The children were huddled in groups trembling and crying looking to Miss Bettie for comfort. Their tear-stained faces reflected their fear. What will we do? Bettie and Mollie held them close and tried to reassure them that God had kept them safe and everything would be alright.

This was not the first tragedy that affected the very existence of the Hephzibah Orphanage. Due to the faith of its founder, Sarah Elizabeth Tyler "Bettie," the Hephzibah Orphanage overcame several misfortunes.

In the beginning, My Great Aunt Bettie, and her sister Mary Ann "Mollie," were deeply involved in the mission work of their church, in Macon, Georgia. However, when their aunt died and left four little boys ages two to eight, they agreed to care for them as their father was having difficulty in caring for them alone.

The two spinster sisters began to pray for answers and guidance and felt that it was from God that they were to move from mission work to working with orphans.

This was the humble beginning of the Hephzibah Orphanage. The name "Hephzibah" was chosen because of its meaning. "His delight is in her," as it is recorded in Isaiah 62: 4.

With four boys now in their care, Bettie realized they had outgrown the original house that she and Mollie had shared, so they went to their knees and prayed for a bigger place. They thought about the old home place with a big farmhouse and six hundred acres in Bolingbroke, Georgia, only ten miles from Macon. The land was mostly timber, and it had been left to the four Tyler children. Bettie's sister and brothers sold their part of the farm to her.

With the timber on the land, she set up a sawmill and had logs cut into lumber to enlarge the orphanage. My grandmother, Chattie Trotman married Willis Tyler, Bettie's brother, and helped raise vegetables to provide for the growing orphan's home. They were now taking in children from broken homes and wards of the state as well as orphans.

In 1904, a tornado passed over the orphanage in Bolingbroke, blowing down houses that were being built for the workers. The children were outside when my grandmother saw the funnel cloud and herded them quickly into the house. The residence was not damaged, and no children nor workers were hurt, so "His delight is in her" confirmed to Bettie that was why the house and children were safe. The orphanage, at times seemed to have obstacles that were insurmountable, but Bettie and Mollie depended on prayer and felt that they were to move to Macon from Bolingbroke in 1906.

The orphanage grew from seventy-five to one hundred children with a school and houses for both boys and girls. My mother and father were house parents for several years. My Aunt Grace, mother's sister cooked on a big wood burning stove making many biscuits for the Hephzibah family.

After the 1916 fire, in which no one was injured, prayer was what Bettie clung to, so down on her knees, she went in prayer. Bettie trusted God again. A few days after the fire, Bettie received a telegram with two thousand dollars from a total stranger in California, who had heard about the fire. Another move! God not only consistently provided a place, but it was always a bigger, better place.

Five years later, in 1921, Aunt Bettie approached the delegation of the Wesleyan Methodist Church and offered them the opportunity to purchase the Hephzibah Orphanage and to continue the principle on which it was founded.

On January 17, 1922, the property was signed over to the Wesleyan Methodist Church. Soon after, due to failing health, Aunt Bettie retired, and without Bettie, Mollie retired within the year. Before Bettie died, in 1928, she felt that God had provided for the Hephzibah to continue to teach high Christian principles.

The Hephzibah Children's Home, as it is known today, is located on Zebulon Road, in Macon, Georgia. The main buildings are an Administration Building, a large modern Dining Hall, individual residences for boys and girls with house parents for every eight to ten children in each home. There is an up to date home for unwed mothers where the mothers are counseled to either keep their babies or give them up for adoption.

In the year 2000, a "100 Year Celebration" was held and some of those in attendance were adults who had been residents as children. Other children residents, now grown, are serving as administrators at the Hephzibah. Many of my family members were present as well.

The original house that Bettie and Mollie shared with the four little boys has been moved to the location on Zebulon Road. It has been preserved in memory of Aunt Bettie and so that visitors could see the early beginnings of the Hephzibah Orphanage.

2017 finds the Hephzibah Children's Home growing and thriving. God has always been and is still faithful to His Word. "HIS DELIGHT IS IN HER" has held true through the years.

Chapter Nine
Historical Memories From 1939-1963
U.S. Presidents

I am privileged to have lived during twelve presidential elections from 1933 to 2017. Three of these presidents have left an indelible memory in my mind.

The first one was President Franklin Delano Roosevelt. The day he died in 1945, I was in fifth grade in Cordele, Georgia. I had ridden my bicycle three blocks to the small neighborhood store to get a snack. While I was looking down the candy aisle, I overheard some men talking about our president. I heard one of them say that the president had died that day. "Our President Roosevelt?" I questioned myself, "Could it be?"

My heart started thumping as I forgot about the candy and jumped on my bicycle and peddled as fast as I could back home. Dropping my bike on the sidewalk, skipping two steps at the time up to the wide front porch, I burst through the front door letting the screen door slam shut. Something I had been cautioned, many times, not to do.

Grandmother seeing the fear on my face asked, "What is wrong?" Catching my breath, I told her that I had heard that President Roosevelt had died. She hurried over to the big floor model mahogany radio and turned it on. We sat together listening to the reporters announcing the devastating news.

As a child, I was frightened as nothing like this had ever happened in my life. I wondered, "What will happen to our country, what will happen to us?" President Roosevelt was highly respected by my family, and I was taught that same respect.

President Roosevelt had been elected to the presidency in 1933, the year I was born. To me, he was MY president.

***

Nothing can erase the emptiness and the unbelief that I experienced that day in 1963 while I was shopping with my six-year-old daughter at Edgewater Shopping Center in Orlando, Florida. It had been an ordinary day when I picked Karyl up after school to shop for hair ribbons for her long blond braids. Walking in McCrory's five and dime store the PA system blared out that President John Fitzgerald Kennedy had been shot and killed while riding in a motorcade in Dallas, Texas.

Karyl

The world seemed to stop turning on its axis. You could hear a pin drop. Silence – dead silence. The shoppers were standing, unmoving. I was numb, not grasping the reality of what I was hearing. Hair ribbons were no longer important. Karyl and I walked to the car and drove home.

When I entered the house, nothing was normal though nothing had physically changed. The air hung heavy. Turning on the television, the first image that came over the screen was of Jackie Kennedy climbing on the back of the open convertible to help her fallen husband.

Sirens blaring, emergency vehicles racing through the streets made the reality come into focus.

President Kennedy won the presidency in 1961. Now in 1963, just two short years, he was gone.

***

The sound of helicopters whirring overhead drew all eyes upward into the clear Florida sky. Marine One helicopter came into view first as the buzzing got closer and louder. Two more helicopters flanked each side of Marine One as it circled directly over the Administration Building of Florida Technological University in Orlando, Florida.

Excitement mounted as the helicopters landed. Seeing the President of the United States, President Richard Nixon, disembark onto our campus was a special day.

The Reflection Pool, in front of the Administration Building, had been drained and chairs replaced the beautiful water of floating lotus flowers for seven hundred graduates that June morning in 1973.

The President of the University, President Millikan, escorted President Nixon onto the platform amid shouts of excitement and applause.

The temperature was in the 90's that day, as, we, the graduates sweltered in our long black gowns along with eight to ten thousand guests.

Before diplomas were issued, President Nixon gave about a thirty-minute positive speech encouraging us to believe in ourselves, the future of our country, and to contribute to its continued leadership in the world.

The day that I received my Bachelor in Arts Degree in Education was a day to remember.

Chapter Ten
World War II: 1939-1945

I was in elementary school in 1942 during the war. Everyone was asked to support the war by collecting any scrap metal that could be recycled into building tanks and airplanes to be used by the military to defend America. Another use of the metal was for weapons.

Me at 9 Years Old

I can still see that scrap metal piled high on the front lawn of my elementary school. Periodically, it would be picked up and taken to be fashioned into a variety of metal or tin products needed by the military.

Army tanks were being built in Lakeland, Florida. I could see trains loaded with Army tanks moving through Lakeland on their way to military posts.

Later, in 1943, when my brother in law was drafted into the Navy, my sister, Loyce, and I and their baby girl, Glenda, moved to Georgia with Aunt Mary.

The government issued Books of Stamps to ration the number of certain products that would assure our troops would have everything they needed. Some of the commodities that were controlled were sugar, meat, shoes and even gasoline.

I remember that we had to use a stamp to buy a pair of shoes and we were only allowed to buy two pairs of shoes in a year. People could use as much gasoline as they needed to drive to work and back home. If you purely drove for pleasure, you were only allowed three gallons of gas each week.

Americans, were very patriotic and were willing to do their part for our country.

V-J DAY – 1945

I was living with Aunt Mary in Cordele, Georgia when sirens sounded along with car horns blaring. Neighbors were calling over the back fences and on the party line telephones to spread the word that it was V- J DAY --VICTORY IN JAPAN! THE WAR WAS OVER!

I ran the eight blocks from my house down to the Main Street in town where I found several hundred people were already lining the sidewalks to watch the parade of cars driving through the streets honking their car horns and waving flags. The atmosphere was electric. Everyone was clapping their hands and shouting, "It's over! The war is over!". Even the little children were jumping up and down. This meant that fathers and brothers, uncles and cousins would be coming home to be with their families again! The celebration continued into the night in many houses, as families gathered together to celebrate with family and neighbors.

Chapter Eleven
Train Ride by Pullman

What would it be like, I wondered, to ride the train and sleep in a Pullman Sleeper car? At sixteen, I had never been north of Atlanta, Georgia. Aunt Mary and I were taking this trip from Cordele, Georgia to Weatherly, Pennsylvania to see my sister, Jenny, and her husband. We had not seen her in two years since she married Sam and moved to Weatherly. Now we were also going to see my new niece, Joycelyn.

The day of departure finally arrived. I was up early even though our train wasn't leaving until six o'clock that evening.

Aunt Mary always wanted us girls to be dressed appropriately for the occasion. In 1948, a girl was expected to wear a dress and have matching accessories when she attended any special event and that included traveling on a train. I was dressed to fit the bill.

Waiting for the train in the small train station in Cordele was just as exciting, to me, as waiting in the train station in Washington D.C., that I had read about in a magazine, with its marble floors and many platforms where passengers wait for boarding.

Anxious for the arrival of the train and watching people milling about, I finally heard the train whistle in the distance. With nerves of excitement, Aunt Mary and I walked outside to the platform. The whistle got closer and we could see the smoke puffing out of the smokestack as it rounded the curve. The brakes screeched to a stop and we walked to the car where the conductor was placing the portable steps down for boarding.

Climbing up the steps, we walked left into the Pullman car. As we walked down the center aisle, looking for the number of our compartment, I noticed that the numbers on the left were even and the numbers on the right were odd. Finding our compartment on the left, we sat in the plush seats and I breathed a sigh of pure pleasure.

About eight o'clock, with the help of the conductor, the seats were converted into double-decker births. Changing into our pj's, Aunt Mary took the lower birth and I climbed into the upper and pulled the heavy curtain closed.

I had probably been up thirteen hours, but this new experience kept me awake. It was a whole different world. After looking at every detail of my birth, I turned off the light and lay there listening to the sounds around me. I drifted off to sleep listening to the hiss of the engine and the clack of the wheels turning on the rails.

The next morning, we awoke to the loud voice of the conductor as he walked down the center aisle of the sleeper car tapping on the compartments on the left and the right, announcing that breakfast was being served in the dining car.

We quickly dressed, walked through two other swaying cars to the dining car. I had a good southern breakfast of grits and egg with thick, crisp bacon. Finishing my orange juice, we walked unsteadily through the same swaying cars back to our compartment where the births had now been converted back to comfortable seats. We relaxed the remainder of the trip.

It was exciting as I had never been this far north before. Jenny's friends introduced me to some young people, my age, who included me in their plans and we spent time swimming at their local park and pool. I enjoyed my first slice of pizza. It was an unfamiliar food in the south.

My southern accent kept them asking me questions to hear me talk. Of course, they didn't realize they had a northern accent that intrigued me.

Spending a week with my sister and her family and especially the beautiful baby girl, Joycelyn, was the highlight of my summer. It was time to say sad goodbyes and return on the train back to Cordele.

Chapter Twelve

Performing

I pulled a hand sewn dress made of polished red cotton over my head that mother, recently diagnosed with cancer, had created for this special occasion. I felt very important. I twirled around to see the gathered skirt open up like an umbrella. Handmade tatting (a kind of knotted lace) sewn by my grandmother accented the Peter Pan collar. Delicately lace-edged socks were folded neatly above my white high-top shoes with their snow-white shoe strings.

Climbing on to a dining room chair with two pillows stacked one on top of the other to put me high enough to have my blonde curls styled like Shirley Temple, the child star in the 1930's who stole the hearts of many Americans by dancing and singing in her many popular movies. I was the same age as Shirley Temple, and with mother's sewing talent, she duplicated many of the clothes that Shirley Temple wore in some of those movies for me.

It was almost time to go to our church Christmas Program, so mother had me practice my four-line poem one more time. She walked me and my six siblings, who all had a part in the program, the three blocks to the church. All of us were excited, knowing that after the program, everyone, even adults would receive a brown bag filled with hard candy, nuts in the shells, raisins still on the stems and a piece of fruit, usually an apple.

The excitement grew when we entered the already half-filled sanctuary. The aroma of the pine boughs topped with red holly berries wrapped around glass globes, with a candle in each, set the mood.

After saying Merry Christmas to our friends, we took our seats as Mrs. Clapp, my Sunday school teacher, started playing "Away in a Manger" on the old upright piano.

When my name was announced, I quickly walked up to the platform with pride and confidence and recited my poem. Curtsying, as I had practiced, I walked back to my seat by my mother who smiled and patted me on the knee. The applause and the many compliments that I received made me feel special. If one can be hooked by reciting a four-line poem, at two years old, then I was hooked.

That was the beginning of my love of performing. Even though I had no formal training, memorizing poetry, monologues and short stories was always a part of my life.

The next three years, performing was not at the top of our list of priorities. My sister, Jenny entertained Betty and me, the two youngest siblings, with walks in the woods, making cupcakes in my Little Orphan Annie electric stove or just keeping us occupied away from the realization of mother's imminent death.

My older siblings, along with Aunt Mary, mother's sister, and our grandmother, kept a close vigil by mother's bed to administer medications, keep her comfortable and more importantly, to spend as much time as possible with her.

With sadness hanging heavy over our home, the ones who understood the gravity of the situation with mother also had to deal with me when I contracted Whooping Cough. Many times, during the day and the night I remember my brother throwing me up over his head forcing me to gasp for air to save my life.

After mother's death, our lives changed rapidly much like a

Ferris wheel when it turns and sometimes pauses at the top. It is there that I was happy and excited. Holding my breath, waiting for the wheel to continue downward, but hoping it wouldn't hesitate at the bottom where I felt fear and uncertainty. I would pray for the wheel to keep turning and bring me back to the top where all fear was gone.

I was eight years old and in the third grade when happiness and a new environment unfolded for me when I moved from Macon, Georgia to Lakeland, Florida with my sister, Loyce, and her new husband, Wesley.

Once again, my sister, Loyce started sharing and performing poetry with me as we had done in the past. Her humorous monologues became some of my favorites. I would deliver "Elmira's Last Beau" anytime, anywhere when asked. "The Crooked Mouth Family" would bring tears from laughter to any audience.

In elementary school, I always volunteered to read aloud when a story required an accent to match the dialogue. The more the kids enjoyed it, the stronger my voice and facial expressions became. Directing my first play, as a sixth grader, kept the fire burning to perform.

In high school, I was soon responding to requests to share some of my stories. I performed in a "1920s" Fashion Show" at the Lakeland City Auditorium.

Later, performing "A Small Boys Troubles" in a high school Talent Show, one of the fathers attending, invited me to perform for the Civitan Club at their next meeting. My principal excused me from class to do it. I walked from the high school the eight blocks to downtown, Lakeland, to the Civitan Club's meeting room upstairs above the S & S Cafeteria. After the men of the Civitan Club expressed their enjoyment of my performance about a young boy in overalls sitting on a turned down bucket going over the unfairness of life on a farm. I walked the eight blocks back to school and my classes.

The lengthy "Little Orphan Annie" poem by James Whitcomb Riley in 1885 was another favorite. Between my school, church, local and family gatherings I was able to share my love of performing through various types of literature.

As a senior in high school, I accepted the challenge of selecting and directing a drama for our church to celebrate the birth of Christ at Christmas time.

Continuing that love, as a teacher, I introduced storytelling and Poetry Alive to my sixth-grade students. To see the pride and pleasure on the faces of my students after they had performed in front of their peers was gratifying to me.

Our local Reading Council was known to set up a makeshift stage in the middle of a shopping mall on a busy Saturday morning to lure shoppers and children to listen to stories performed by the council members. My rendition of "Medio Polito" or "Little Half-Chick" told with a Spanish accent appealed to many with a Latin background. Everyone loves a good story especially one that was a favorite as a child. As a Reading Specialist, my purpose was to draw attention and interest in reading.

A group of teachers, including myself, formed a Teachers Theatre Group, performing plays for the students and the community. The success of our first performance "In the Still of The Night" encouraged us to continue to perform a play each spring. A fellow teacher, Mary Schiano, performed live music for each and every production. With each performance, more teachers joined the group for the next production. The teachers gave many

Me in "South Pacific"

hours after school rehearsing for "Yankee Doodle," "South Pacific," "Our Miss Brooks" and "The 1940's Radio Hour". to name a few

Our middle school soon gained the reputation, in jest, that, in order to get a job there, you had to act, sing, dance or play a musical instrument. Our principal, Rick Mossman, was in many productions himself.

Me in "Yankee Doodle"

Retiring from teaching and moving to North Carolina, I discovered the Smokey Mountain Center for the Performing Arts. Not a professional performer, I boldly approached the owner and director of the Overlook Theatre, Scotty Corbin, introduced myself and expressed my interest in performing. Later, I auditioned for and was cast in "Annie." That began my relationship with the Overlook Theatre. For the next six years, I performed in a number of productions. Storytelling has been another way that I performed with the theatre. I performed Uncle

Remus's story of "Tar Baby" on one occasion. At the age of eighty-two, I chose
to perform in "Shriek" for my last show
with the Overlook Theatre. However, the
following year, I was asked to share a
Christmas story "Francie Nolan's Christmas Tree" in the Theatre's Christmas
Variety show.

Me, Shrek

Nikki Corbin, Scotty's wife, provid-
ed slides to coincide with the story in my original monologue,
"Freedom," that I performed in the Macon County Senior Follies
winning the Bronze Medal.

Scotty, Nikki, and Me in
Shrek

Whether it was performing an original monologue with the Senior Follies or
volunteering as an usher for the Smokey
Mountain Center for the Performing
Arts, I have special memories today of
those experiences and the people I met.

Every role that I had with the Overlook Theatre, not only allowed me to
learn and grow, but it also wove another
thread into my life's tapestry.

Today, I consider that every phase of my life has molded me
into the person I am. I feel blessed for the many opportunities that
God has allowed me, a simple, southern girl to experience.

Chapter Thirteen
Future Husband

The first time I saw my future husband, Jim, we were both eight years old. He remembers that he met me at my house when he attended a young boys club held there. Jim insists that he fell in love with me then. It was my blonde hair. He says that it shone like the sun. (That shine came after every shampooing, as my hair was rinsed with either lemon juice or vinegar.)

Jim was shy and never drew attention to himself. We were different in many ways. I never met a stranger. I would talk to anyone. At that age, I wasn't into boys. I was a little bit tom-boyish. I loved climbing the plum tree in the backyard where I would sit and eat juicy, sweet, purple plums.

Sometimes I walked gingerly on the top rail of the chain link fence around our yard pretending to be a high wire performer. A chain-link fence was different in the 1940's than they are today. Back then, the vertical posts and top rails were made of wood, and the metal chain link fence was attached to that. Our posts were

Jim in Uniform

painted green, and the horizontal railing was three inches wide, making it easy for me to walk across. I tore more than one dress with lace and ruffles that my sister had made for me, on that fence. She was very tolerant of my shenanigans.

I was nine years old during World War II, and metal was needed for building supplies for our military. Schools even had metal drives with the students scouring their neighborhoods and bringing any metal and iron objects that they could find. I vividly remember the enormous pile of scrap metal in the schoolyard. Women worked in the factory in Lakeland to build tanks for the war.

It was during that war that I moved back to Georgia with Aunt Mary and Uncle Warren. Now, Loyce and their new baby girl could be near her husband as he had been drafted into the Navy and was stationed from Great Lakes, Illinois to Key West, Florida. Wesley was discharged from the Navy soon after his ship sank, in a typhoon, in the South Pacific. I moved back to Lakeland and life resumed as usual.

Jim was, now, back in the picture. We both attended John Cox Elementary School. We were never in the same classroom and saw each other only at a distance except at church. I didn't give him much thought, but he was still around. He was getting taller and continued to be a neat dresser. His hair was always parted and combed to the side.

Two years of Junior High School was a change for both of us. I met new friends who occupied my time. However not seeing him as often, didn't mean I excluded him as a friend. He was still a friend, and I did notice how his dimples dipped deep into his cheeks when he smiled.

In high school, I was involved with The Classical (Latin) Club and a service club, Y-Teens. I was also active in soccer and softball. After a soccer game, I found out he had been making a movie of the game just to see me play. I don't think they called it stalking back then.

Walking home from school one afternoon in the hot Florida

sun, Jim was already there when I arrived. After cooling off with a nice cold glass of sweet tea, he asked if he could take a few pictures of me with his new camera. I wasn't really in the mood to sit for photos, but not wanting to be rude, I consented. I needed to freshen up and touch up my hair after my long walk home in the heat.

Hanging a piece of blue velvet fabric between the living room and the dining room, he had me pose sitting on a vanity stool with the velvet as the backdrop.

Bringing the developed pictures over one evening, I knew he probably would not consider that as a profession, but he could enjoy it as a hobby. I was staring at the camera like a deer in the headlights with that blue velvet hanging loosely behind me. Then, I learned that the fabric had come out of a hearse. I was not charmed by any of this, but he was still nice.

In high school, I was dating Jim's best friend, Bill. Both of them played on the high school football team. When Bill came over to the house, Jim would show up, and I would get annoyed with him. Today, Jim denies knowing that Bill was there. There are always two sides to every story.

During the Homecoming Football Game, Bill chose me as his girlfriend to ride around the field at halftime in a convertible. I wore a stylish forest green wool suit with a large round collar. My blouse, made of soft gold silk with smocking around the neck, accented the green color nicely. My shoulder length hair blew in the cool October breeze.

I had to walk, over a mile, to school but Jim drove his sister's car. He admits that he used to drive about a block from my house and park and wait until he saw me coming. Then he would back up and ask if I wanted a ride. Of course, I would ride, I was carrying a stack of heavy books. Book bags were not popular in the 1950's.

We graduated from high school in 1952 and Bill went away to college. I didn't have the finances to go right after high school, so I started working in a finance office in Lakeland. Making my own money was important to me. I never asked my family for money. I never had to, as they gave me the things I needed.

Forty dollars a week for my first job taking shorthand and running a cash drawer gave me a feeling of independence. I paid my sister ten dollars a week for room and board. That ten dollars a week included a nice bedroom, three meals a day and I am not proud to say that my sister even did my laundry

With Bill at Emory studying to be a surgeon, I eventually accepted a date with Jim. It wasn't long before I began noticing his good qualities and the similarities in our backgrounds. He was next to the youngest of twelve children, and I was the youngest of nine. My father died before I was born, and his father died when he was four. We had the same Christian values and family was important to both of us. The more we dated and spent time together, the more I knew that I loved him.

When he was drafted into the Army, during the Korean War, I would wait anxiously on Saturdays to see if he would be able to come home for the weekend from the Army base in Ft. Benning, Georgia where he was stationed. My heart would drop when he didn't make it. Our love was sure, and one night when bringing

Me after engagement

me home from a date, he gave me a goodnight kiss. While he was stationed at Ft. Benning, we decided to get married in our childhood church in Lakeland.

Chapter Fourteen
Our Wedding

Our wedding would be small, and I would pay for it myself. I knew immediately that my maid of honor would be, Gloria, a very close friend, and her sister Bobbie would be my bridesmaid with my niece, Glenda as the junior bridesmaid. My two-year-old niece, Gail was to be the flower girl. Jim's brothers were the groomsmen and best man. My brother-in-law, Wesley gave me away.

Me at my wedding, 1954

My dress was made, by the mother of my bridesmaids, out of white faille material. It was ballerina length with two-inch scallops beginning at the neckline down the full span of the gown with a wide lace insert. The round neck had a lace peter pan collar, and the long-tapered sleeves were gathered at the shoulder under a scalloped cap. My headpiece was scalloped lace attached to tulle fabric designed with scallops around the edge of the mid-length veil.

I wore white satin pumps and carried a white Bible with one white orchid and babies breath tied with a narrow white ribbon. The church was decorated with large arrangements of Lilies of the Valley flanked by a candelabra on each side of the altar. My brother, Reverend Harold Hampton, officiated at our wedding ceremony on December 29, 1954.

My attendants wore long taffeta dresses in pastel colors of pink, lavender, and mint green. Their headpieces were made of small silk flowers, and they carried bouquets of mixed fresh blossoms. My Aunt Katherine sang "The Sweetest Story Ever Told" and "I Love You Truly". A friend from work played the "Traditional Wedding March" on the piano.

The music started and my brother-in-law, Wesley, extended his arm for me to place my arm under his. I was excited but nervous. When I saw Jim look back waiting for me to approach the altar, flashing me a smile, I relaxed and returned the smile.

Jim at our wedding, 1954

As Wesley gave me away, I stood beside him with pride. Our vows, read by my brother, Harold, were repeated clearly by both of us. When we were pronounced man and wife, Jim lifted my veil and gave me a tender kiss.

We took a short honeymoon to Miami, Florida where we enjoyed some of the sights and drove on the beach which was beautiful and especially warm for December. The sandy beach was not as white as the beach at Daytona where my family spent a lot of time in the summer.

When we returned, the finance office, where I worked, transferred me to their division in Columbus, Georgia near where Jim was stationed at Fort Benning. After two years, Jim was ready to deploy to Korea and I was planning to go back to Lakeland to wait for him. However, the war ended just two weeks before he was to leave. Soon after, he was discharged, and we went home together. I transferred back to my old office where I continued working until two months before our first child was born in 1957. Jim has always been a loving and supportive husband and has never wavered from his Christian values. He is still a quiet and mild-mannered, patient man. We were married 63 years in December 2017.

Jim and Bill were friends after Bill finished medical school, but lost contact with him for several years. Learning that he had passed away and that he had lived within ten miles from us, Jim was able to attend his funeral and spoke at the service. Later, Jim talked with Bill's son and was able to share stories and pictures of him.

Our Wedding Party: Glenda, Bobbie, Gloria, Me, Jim and
C.W.

Chapter Fifteen
Children

We resettled in Lakeland after Jim's discharge from the Army in July 1956. Our first child was born a normal, healthy girl, Annette Karyl on March 9, 1957. She was a very precocious child who often surprised us with her antics and her abilities. Learning to walk at nine months gave her the mobility to travel faster and find more things to explore. She learned, at a young age that she could open the chain lock on the door with the broom handle. She was able to escape once, while I was in another part of the house, but a neighbor caught her quickly and brought her home.

Karyl at 7 months old

I won't say that Karyl was clumsy, I'll just say she was not well coordinated. It seemed, at every meal, she would turn her cup of milk over at least twice. We obviously talked about it to the point, that it made a big impression on her. Sometime later, it was evident that she had not forgotten about it.

Karyl at 5 years

Her vocabulary grew quickly, and as I loved memorizing poetry from a young age, I started teaching her verses from the Bible. At two she was memorizing scripture from the 23rd Psalm. When reciting the fifth verse for her daddy, one

70

day, she said it perfectly until she got down to, "my cup runneth over" when she said, "Goodness gracious, I spilled over my cup." We knew, then, that we had put too much emphasis on her spilling her milk.

She was also a child who was very observant and very vocal. She told everything she knew or everything she thought she knew. Therefore, it was wise for us to talk with caution around her.

I was driving to my sister's house in Lakeland from Orlando when Karyl was five. When the highway patrolman's blue light got my attention, I realized I was speeding. So, I pulled over and stopped. The officer noticed from my driver's license that I lived in Altamonte Springs, just as some of his family did. He then talked about the small town and advised me to slow down. Thankfully, he did not give me a ticket.

Knowing Karyl, I told her not to mention the incident to Aunt Loyce, (that was my mistake) as there was nothing to tell. She agreed,

Jimmy at 4 months old

but when I pulled into Aunt Loyce's driveway before I had even stopped, she opened her car door before I came to a complete stop and shouted to the top of her lungs, "We almost got put in jail!" for all the neighbors to hear. That was Karyl! My sister was completely unnerved until I could explain the truth.

Karyl continued to entertain us, and when she was three, we welcomed our second child, a boy, James Preston II (Jimmy), May 28, 1960.

Jimmy was the first boy born into our family in twenty-eight years. We are very proud of the ten boys and girls that my brother and nieces and nephews adopted. Each one is a blessing to our family.

Jimmy was a healthy looking, very active little boy with soft light

brown ringlets that covered his head and bounced when he ran. He kept surprising us with some unusual issues that you would never imagine until they happened.

Karyl at 4 years old and Jimmy at 1 year old

When he was seven, his legs were paralyzed from a severe case of Strep infection. He was hospitalized in ICU for several days before it was diagnosed. Many prayers were answered, and he regained the use of his legs. God was always there.

The next hurdle for him was double vision. He would invariably ride his bike into a pothole, in the road, not being able to tell which of the two potholes was real. Wearing a patch over one eye, doing eye exercises, and wearing little black rimmed glasses, that made him look very studious, did not change the double vision. Eventually, surgery helped, but it is very difficult to clip a muscle in one eye to match the exact length of the muscle in the other eye.

As a young teen, Jimmy had a pinto horse named Betty that was very gentle. He could ride her lying across her back with feet dangling down one side and she would walk him home over the dirt roads behind our house and the golf course.

Soon after, Karyl got a horse, but she was not very athletic; actually, she was not athletic at all. She was better at singing and playing the piano.

Jimmy was more athletic than his sister, but they both had horses and enjoyed riding. Jimmy, having a more spirited horse, (he named her Figure), was warned not to ride her without a tie-down because she had been used to racing. A tie-down is a strap that keeps the horse's head at a level that enables the rider to control the horse's movements. Choosing to ride her bareback, against our warning, Figure got her head up and bolted across a busy highway just missing a car. She went down dragging Jimmy across the road leaving asphalt in his feet for weeks. Thinking that he would eventually grow up and listen to his dad's wise advice, we continued to love him and asked God to protect him.

Jimmy at 7 years old

Riding a dirt bike was just as disastrous for him. Once maneuvering a jump in the woods, miles from home, his engine stalled sending him and his cycle into a nosedive. He landed in the path of his friend riding behind him. The friend missed landing on Jimmy's head by inches. His friend carried him, with broken bones, on the back of his dirt bike to the hospital. After being patched up at the hospital, Jimmy insisted on leaving the ER. So, his friend brought him home. We were out of town that day. When we got home, we found a mangled son in a lot of pain, in a full leg cast, walking with a cane, who refused to admit that he needed help.

He actually lived to be an adult. Thankfully, God never gives up on us. Today, he builds U.S. Embassies and Consulates in different countries and prefers to be called J.P. as he doesn't think "Jimmy" sounds appropriate for a Project Manager or Senior Superintendent of a U.S. Government project.

Chapter Sixteen

Laughter is the Best Medicine

Even though Jimmy had a number of health and accident issues, he was a funny little kid.

Any time our toddler, Jimmy, was quiet I started looking for him. Knowing that he was in the house, I peeked into each room until I saw him in the kitchen holding a bottle of chocolate syrup upside down with a pool of chocolate on the floor.

In one hand he had Karyl's crepe paper pompom trying to mop it up. When he saw me, he ran dragging the chocolate  covered pompom across the kitchen floor, through the dining room, across the living room and circling back to the kitchen through our bedroom. His short little legs moved faster than mine. Catching him was not easy but cleaning up the trail of chocolate was worse.

* * *

Jimmy at 3 years old

Jimmy had a winsome smile that served him well in some awkward situations. One busy day, trying to finish straightening up the house I told him to pick up his toys and put them in the toy box. As he turned to walk away, he said, "Not now, I'm busy." I think he felt the tension because he looked back. When he saw the look on my face, he knew he had said the wrong thing. I just looked at him in disbelief trying to decide how to respond. Then he looked up at me with a slight grin and said, "I'll kiss you. Will that be alright"?

He won!

* * *

One beautiful summer day, with the temperature in the 90's, we planned a picnic in the park. While Jim was loading the car with water toys and chairs, I was packing a lunch of peanut butter and jelly sandwiches along with chips and a thermos filled with good cold lemonade.

Jimmy was standing by the ice chest full of crushed ice. When I saw him, he was putting the ice in the aquarium with the tropical fish, I Yelled, "No!" Then I saw a little angelfish floating on its back near the top. I put my hand under the tiny frozen fish. I was sure that it was dead, but suddenly there was a slight movement of its tail, and it swam away.

The crushed ice melted quickly, and we were able to save the rest of the fish Jimmy showed remorse over almost losing all of his fish. The fun at the park was worth the anxiety of getting there.

* * *

After everyone had opened their gifts Christmas morning, Jimmy saw the present for his cat still under the tree. Grabbing it, he ran looking for Fluffy. Not finding her, he had all the cousins searching for her but to no avail. Being persistent, he ran into the house and got a little horn that he had just gotten for Christmas.

Soon he shouted, "I found her, but she won't wake up." As I stepped outside, I saw him blowing his horn in her ear over and over. Sadly, it was obvious that Fluffy was not going to wake up.

After dinner, we had a funeral for her on Christmas Day. Jimmy played Taps on his horn for his special pet. He seemed satisfied that she was in heaven.

* * *

Driving to church one Sunday morning, five-year-old Jimmy surprised me when he asked, "Is our preacher rich"? Not expecting that, I said, "I don't know. Why do you want to know?" He said, "Well, he takes the offering every Sunday, and he doesn't share with the rest of us." "Out of the mouths of Babes!"

* * *

Jasper was a kitten that a friend had given to the children. Jimmy was young and had never had a kitten. He was completely absorbed with him. The little kitten, would purr and mew when he held him. Bringing the kitten to me, he said, "Jasper is hungry." I told him that he wasn't hungry, he had already had his dinner. He sat down nearby and said again that Jasper was hungry. After this same conversation the third time, I finally said, "Why do you think he is hungry?" Jimmy replied, "He keeps saying mii--lk, mii--lk." There was nothing for me to do, but give Jasper some mii-lk.

* * *

Jimmy kept every day interesting with actions that no one could have possibly imagined beforehand.

A 2' x 3' metal grate covered the top of the oil floor furnace that was located in the hallway in the center of the house. Of course, our toddler, Jimmy was fascinated with it. The little square holes in the grate were a temptation and filling them up was a challenge. He discovered that my belts fit through the holes easily, so that was the next best thing. I learned that if a belt was missing, I would get out the vacuum cleaner and it could be retrieved with the powerful suction of the vacuum.

In the summertime, when the furnace was not being used, it

was not difficult to retrieve objects that had been dropped through the holes. However, in winter, when the furnace was hot, we had a bigger problem.

One cold February day, Jimmy deposited something that could not be retrieved with the vacuum. Soon a stench filled the house. Oh no! Where was that boy? He was standing by the furnace with wearing only his long sleeve shirt.

After putting coats and hats on both children and opening all the windows, I called Jim and explained my dilemma and asked him to bring all the air fresheners, he could find, as soon as possible.

When Jim got home, he understood the emergency. However, the air fresheners were not effective. There was nothing to do but wait until the furnace burned off that strange little-wet sprinkle that caused the furnace to cough up that horrible odor.

* * *

Living on a golf course gave us some moments of pleasure, grief, and humor. Learning the etiquette of golf was not easy for a two-year-old.

Entertaining friends in the backyard by the pool, I heard a commotion out front. One of the little girls was saying, "Run in the house, Jimmy!" Run in the house!" Getting up to investigate, a lady carrying a golf club was running from our front yard around to the back. I asked her if I could help her. In a very agitated voice, she said, "That little boy got my golf ball."

Going out front with the stranger following me, I saw - guess who - Yep! Jimmy holding a golf ball. When I asked him where he got it, he said, "In the road." The lady confirmed that she hit it in the road and he picked it up.

I instructed him to give the lady her ball. After apologizing, I told her I could assure her he would not pick up any more of her golf balls.

Jimmy was two, and in retrospect, it was a little bit humorous to see a grown lady chasing a two-year-old around the block to retrieve a golf ball.

* * *

Only a dirt road separated our front yard from the third fairway of the eighteen-hole golf course in Altamonte Springs, Florida. I was accustomed to rude golfers beating my azaleas with their golf clubs looking for the golf balls that they had sliced from the third tee just fifty feet from our yard.

One warm day, Rascal, our family dog was sleeping near the bushes when a golfer came into the yard poking around the blooming azaleas. When he got too close, Rascal growled a warning to him. Still determined to get his ball, he swung his club at Rascal. Now, Rascal decided it was time to go into guard dog mode. The man realized his mistake and ran hopping onto his golf cart with Rascal at his heels. The golfer was safe, but Rascal got a bite out so his" treasured" golf bag.

Yes, our insurance bought the "gentleman" a new golf bag, but I don't remember seeing him up close again.

Chapter Seventeen
Cape Kennedy

Living in Florida and only a forty-five-minute drive to Cape Kennedy, we were privileged to witness a number of rocket launches. Some were during the day, and others were at night. A daytime launch was an amazing sight when a rocket launched into a clear sky. The naked eye could see the rocket and the trail of white smoke until it separated from the booster. It would curve to the left and would soon be out of sight.

Night launches were visible for miles. While waiting for a launch from the parking lot of Jim's store, there was a feeling of anticipation. When we heard "lift off" over the radio, that we were tuned to while waiting, our eyes turned in the direction of the Cape. The sky would have a brilliant orange glow at first; then; we could see the fire shooting from the tail of the rocket until it disappeared into the night sky. Finally, after it vanished, there was a sigh of relief for the safe launch.

Of all the launches that I have seen either live or on television, there are five that are the most memorable to me. Two were disasters, one was a near disaster, and two were perfectly launched rockets to the moon.

Apollo VIII

On December 21, 1968, Apollo VIII was launched with three astronauts on board for the flight to the moon. Colonel Frank Borman as Commander in Chief, along with Captain James Lovell and Major William Andes circled the moon.

While many people question the existence of God, on Christmas Eve December 24, 1968, while in space, each astronaut read in turn from the King James Version, Genesis 1: 1-10 as quoted below:

1. In the beginning God created the heaven and the earth.

2. And the earth was without form, and void; and darkness was upon the face of the deep. And the Spirit of God moved upon the face of the waters.

3. And God said, let there be light: and there was light.

4. And God saw the light, that it was good: and God divided the light from the darkness.

5. And God called the light Day, and the darkness he called Night. And the evening and the morning were the first day.

6. And God said, let there be a firmament in the midst of the waters, and let it divide the waters from the waters.

7. And God made the firmament, and divided the waters which were under the firmament from the waters which were above the firmament: and it was so.

8. And God called the firmament Heaven. And the evening and the morning were the second day.

9. And God said, let the waters under the heaven be gathered together unto one place, and let the dry land appear: and it was so.

10. And God called the dry land Earth; and the gathering together of the waters called he Seas: and God saw that it was good.

My mother-in-law, Cornelia Kinsey wrote a letter to Frank Borman, the Commander in Chief of Apollo VIII telling him that she would be praying for the crew while they were on their mission to the moon. When the astronauts returned to earth, Frank Borman Wrote a personal letter to my mother-in-law thanking her for her

NATIONAL AERONAUTICS AND SPACE ADMINISTRATION
MANNED SPACECRAFT CENTER
HOUSTON, TEXAS   77058

APR 1 5 1969

Mrs. Cornelia Kinsey
2322 Golfview Street
Lake Land, Florida 33801

Dear Mrs. Kinsey:

Many thanks for your congratulations extended on the
successful completion of the Apollo VIII flight. As
a crewman of this historic first voyage around the
moon, I am especially appreciative of your prayers
which you offered in our behalf; and for your kind and
generous comments regarding the Christmas Eve message
which we broadcasted to the people of the good, good
earth, I am deeply grateful.

May the remainder of 1969 bring to you and yours much
happiness and good cheer.

Sincerely,

Frank Borman
Colonel, USAF
NASA Astronaut

prayers while they were in space.

Apollo 13

Apollo 13 was a near disaster, launched on April 1970, when an oxygen tank ruptured damaging power for electrical and life support. After a number of failed attempts to assure the safe return, the astronauts' future was grim. Ground control was running out of options when Jim Lovell, the commander of the crew, used a simple pencil, as a last resort, to fix the problem and saved all three lives on board. It was an agonizing few minutes for all of us. Many prayers were answered that day for their safe return. The movie, Apollo, was made about this rocket launch.

Apollo-Saturn

Another rocket launch, Apollo-Saturn, was the worst disaster in rocket history in the United States at the time. The rocket was on the launch pad. It was a training mission with three astronauts on board. Gus Grissom was the commander. Ed White and Roger Caffee were on their first mission. All three astronauts were inside the rocket when a fire broke out in the cabin. At the time, there was no escape route. The hatch could not be opened from the inside. We could hear the terrifying pleas to get them out. It was the most horrifying sound that I would never forget.

Gus said before they got into the cabin that "One day there would be a disaster and the people would say we had to continue." What a prophetic statement!

Apollo 11

When I got home one evening from taking a class at the college, Jim and the kids met me with the news that they were packed and ready to drive over to Cape Kennedy to see the moon launch the next morning. My husband is a very spontaneous person, so I was not surprised at the sudden plan to see the moon shot. When we got on highway fifty that leads to Cape Kennedy, cars looked like a line of giant ants crawling in a line, searching for a picnic that stretched for several miles. We eased into the traffic and joined the parade.

When we finally arrived at the cape, thousands of people were already there. It was an electrifying atmosphere. Neither the darkness nor the lateness of the hour dampened our excitement. Not many people slept, but we spread our blankets out along the road, across from the launch pad, with hundreds of strangers that quickly became friends. I do not recall getting any sleep as people were milling around all night. As soon as light began to break the horizon, we rolled up our blankets and put them in the car. Then we proceeded to Eckerd Drug Store where we had access to their rooftop to watch the launch. We had to climb an inside ladder, attached to the wall, to get to the roof. I had envisioned stairs not a ladder, but I trudged up not wanting to look like I was afraid, but I am intimidated by height. Once on the roof, I felt safe. I tried not to think about going down.

As Apollo 11 lifted into the sky with Neal Armstrong and Ed Aldrin aboard, it was an indescribable spectacular scene against the brilliant glow of the sunrise over the water. To be a part of such a historical event truly is special. They landed successfully and safely on the moon July 16, 1969.

A friend worked with the company in Orlando that developed

all of NASA's film and gave our son, Jimmy, a 10x20 print of Neil Armstrong walking on the moon from the original NASA film from the moon. It has been professionally framed and is a special memory of that day.

Challenger

Challenger was scheduled to lift off in the morning of January 28, 1986. School was in session that day, and teachers and students were excited about this particular rocket launch as Christa McAuliffe, a science teacher, had been selected from many applicants to be aboard the Challenger.

It was a frigid morning with icicles hanging from the launch tower. As time drew near for liftoff, I took my students outside to watch the launch. After several minutes we were notified by the front office that there was a delay, so we went back inside disappointed. We went out several times and each time the lift off was delayed. There was a two-hour delay due to the ice and fire-protection device. We returned to class again. By the time the students settled down, it was time for lunch. Many students were eating outside when Challenger lifted off. Only 73 seconds into liftoff, the cheers of family and friends turned to cries as pieces of Challenger fell to the ground. The view of a spider-shaped cloud left an indelible mark in all the minds of those watching. It was the worst experience of my life until the collapse of the Twin Towers in September 2001.

I had to change lesson plans that day in order to allow students time to process what they had just witnessed. There were tears, questions, and blank stares. Nothing was normal the rest of the day with students or teachers.

Chapter Eighteen

The Joys of Family Camping

Camping was something we, as a family, had never done, so we decided to go to the mountains of North Carolina as our first camping experience. The brochures on Standing Indian Campground in North Carolina looked like the place for us to start.

My husband purchased all the equipment that he thought we would need. We loaded the car and two children, Jimmy 6 and Karyl 9 and drove from Orlando, Florida to North Carolina. We Arrived at Standing Indian early in the afternoon.

Excitement overruled our common sense as we walked over the wet ground, soaked from an earlier rain, looking for dry firewood. That was the first clue that we were not seasoned campers. A few dry pieces were found so Jim could start a fire for roasting wieners and marshmallows. The book of matches exploded in his hand burning four fingers as he attempted to strike a match. How smart is that? A book of matches to start a fire?

Oh, well, with supper over and our campfire out, we put up our tent on the campsite by the stream. The sun was getting low in the summer sky. Getting our air mattresses and sleeping bags situated in the tent, the children had to try them out. What fun! They were actually going to sleep in a tent, something they had never done.

Finally, as the sun disappeared behind the tall mountain and the stars started to twinkle up above, two tired children began to nod. Everyone snuggled into their sleeping bag, and it wasn't long before the sounds of sleep were evident.

Soon after, thinking everything was perfect, I heard hands slapping and swatting. The children started complaining that something was biting them. Soon I began feeling it too. We slid down into our sleeping bags trying to cover our heads, but nothing we did stopped the torment. Giving up, we finally drifted into a restless sleep.

About an hour later into sleep, Karyl woke with a nosebleed. How fun, looking for tissue by flashlight. With the nosebleed contained, all settled down, and it was quiet again. I am lying there with the strangest feeling that my head was lower than my feet. That couldn't be possible because I was not lying with my head downward on a hill. But unable to concentrate, I finally told my husband how I felt. He examined my air mattress and discovered that mine was designed with a slant downward for my feet, and Yes, I had my head where my feet should have been.

Oh, No! Did Jimmy say he had to go to the bathroom? Never before had he been told it would be alright to relieve himself out-doors in the bushes. He refused to go outside. Now what? Do I take him to the bathroom? No! I do not like going out in the dark by myself. If Jim goes with him, that will leave me here alone with Karyl.

The only solution to this is that we all will have to go. Waking up everyone, I announced that we are all going to the bathroom whether you need to go or not. Getting into a military-style lineup, we all traipse to the restroom two blocks away.

Being the seasoned camper that I am, I rubbed my hand against the wall just inside the door trying to find a light switch. What? No light? How can anyone go to the bathroom in the dark? Jimmy and Karyl both laughed at that brilliant remark.

After all had used the facility in the dark, we began our trek back to the tent. About halfway back, I spied our car, just sitting there empty and lonely. It had soft seats and windows to keep out flying insects. I quickened my footsteps as I thought this could be the answer to getting a little bit of sleep as opposed to more unrest in the tent. Jim had the same idea about the same time I did. We herded the kids into the back door with Karyl on the backseat while Jimmy crawled onto the floor. I jumped into the front passenger seat and felt a sigh of relief. Jim slid into the driver's seat. Everyone settled, and sleep came easy. It wasn't long before Jim fell asleep and his head dropped with a thud on the car horn. Yes! At two A.M.!

We will never know how many campers had anxiety attacks. When the sun rose slowly over the mountain peaks, we thought it wise to pack our camping gear into the car and leave Standing Indian for those with more endurance for camping.

Chapter Nineteen

History in Dramas

Planning a different vacation one summer, we scheduled several Outdoor Dramas in some of the eastern states.

First, we drove to Boone, North Carolina to see "Horn in the West," the story of Daniel Boone during the Revolutionary War and the move west to the Blue Ridge Mountains. The theatre was nestled into the woods high on the mountain with rough cut benches and a small stage. Tree branches made a canape for a roof. The highlight of this for the kids was that Jim was chosen from the audience to be a part of the cast.

The next day, we drove to Radford Virginia to see "The Long Way Home." Arriving early in the afternoon, we drove out to the theatre to find its location. It was a small outdoor theatre with hand-hewn wooden benches with no back support and no overhead covering.

An older lady was there sprucing up the grounds for the show that evening. We learned that she was playing the role of her great-grandmother in the drama that evening. It is the story of Mary Draper Ingles who was captured by the Shawnee Indians when she was twenty-three years old and pregnant. The Indians took her away into the north country leaving most of her family dead and the homestead burned. After being forced to walk for days through rough terrain and losing her child, she lived with the Indians for two years. She was able to escape and found her way back home by following the New River.

The highlight of this afternoon was that Mrs. Ingles invited us to tour her home and explained how her great, great, grandson had built the house with some of its unique features. He had fortified the front door by placing the outside boards on a slant and then arranging the inside boards of the door on a slant in the opposite direction. This was to stop the Indian arrows from penetrating through the door. She, then, invited us to meet the cast after the show. Karyl was excited to see the makeup room and Jimmy's interest was in the costumes, especially the Indian costumes and props.

Next, we drove to Beckley, Virginia to see two dramas performed in the same outdoor Amphitheatre. First, we saw "Honey in the Rock" that took place during the Civil War and is the story of how the birth of the state of West Virginia was born.

The following night, we saw "The Hatfield's and McCoy's," the story of a feud between two rural families in the West Virginia - Kentucky area.

On our way home to Florida, we stopped to see "The Cross and the Sword" in St. Augustine Florida which depicts the story of the first Spanish settlement in Florida.

We all agreed that learning the history of each of the dramas as well as traveling through the different states made a great vacation.

Chapter Twenty
Disney World

Karyl and Jimmy hearing their dad's car pull in the driveway, ran through the kitchen each one trying to get to him first. Their dad had called earlier and said he had a surprise for them when he came home.

Before his dad could get out of the car, Jimmy yelled. "What is the surprise?"

Jim had a big smile on his face. When he got them to settle down, he said, "Well, remember how we have been hearing that Walt Disney is building a theme park near here?"

"Yes," said Karyl. "We have been hearing about that for a long time."

"I know," Jim said. "It is finally opening in two weeks.

"Wow! Can we go when it opens?" Asked Jimmy.

"Better than that," said Jim. "Mr. Disney has invited all the managers and their families, from my company, to come to the Preview Opening the night before Disney World opens to the public.

Ten-year-old Jimmy asked, "Are we famous?"

"No, we are not famous. We are just fortunate to have been invited to the Preview Opening," answered Jim.

"But, there is more," he said.

"What?" Asked Jimmy.

"Well, not only do we get to go, but all shows, rides, and food are complimentary."

"What does complimentary mean?"

"It means it is free - no charge, silly, answered Karyl. She had been quiet up to now, but she asked if she could invite her friend, Connie to go with us. Connie's family had taken Karyl with them to their cabin in upstate New York last Thanksgiving, and they had visited the White House in D. C. on the way up.

Jim agreed that she should invite Connie to go with us. Karyl couldn't wait to tell her. Much discussion, excitement, and speculation about what it would be like ensued.

When the time finally arrived, we drove the twenty miles from our house in Altamonte Springs south on Interstate-4 to the Exit marked Disney World.

Excitement is a mild word to describe the three children in the back seat when they saw the signs leading to the parking lot. We were directed to the "Goofy" parking lot. Riding a tram to the monorail, we waited in line with many other families with children just as excited as we were.

Riding the monorail was a delight in its self, but when I walked through the main gate onto Main Street, I could never have visualized nor imagined the creative genius of Walt Disney.

The beauty and splendor of every detail filled my eyes with wonder. Millions of lights illuminated every tree and manicured shrub.

Mickey Mouse and Minnie delighted the children and allowed photographs to be taken with them. Goofy and Pluto were dancing and entertaining the crowd. The music made the atmosphere electric with excitement.

I said, "Where do we start"? to no one in particular. I just followed the crowd toward Cinderella's Castle. I saw faces with signs of unbelief as I entered into its magic.

The enchantment of the castle captured even Jimmy's attention. Karyl and Connie were mesmerized.

The carousel, Dumbo, and the Tea Cup ride greeted us first. After each child picked the ride of their choice, we mosied over to have a yummy juicy hamburger with fries and a coke.

I noticed that Jim seemed to be focused on the architecture of the buildings and the design of the rides. He is very creative himself, and I could see the wheels turning and wondered what he was thinking. I was intrigued by the detail involved in every animated character in "It's A Small World."

Leaving the castle area, we walked around to the Hall of Presidents, where life-size figures of the Presidents of the United States moved and talked via auto-animatronic technology. We were all amazed at the movements looking so real.

When the tower clock struck twelve midnight, we started back to Main Street to stop by the Candy Shoppe for some sweet treats for the ride home. Of course, each child needed a souvenir to remember this night.

As we left Main Street, we decided to ride the boat across the lagoon back to the parking lots. Disembarking from the boat, we caught a tram that took us back to the "Goofy" parking lot where we spent five minutes looking for our car.

Karyl and Connie both chose It's a Small World for their favorite thing of the evening while Jimmy chose Mr. Toad's Wild Ride and The Country Bear's Jamboree. It was a night to remember.

We purchased our first annual passes to Disney World that year in 1971 for $35.00. We held annual passes for the next thirty years and used them regularly until we moved to North Carolina in 2001.

Chapter Twenty-One
Mountain Cabin

Buying several acres of land, from a young family, on top of their mountain near Burnsville, North Carolina, Jim's creative nature overshadowed his normal thought process. Seeing an old log building falling apart from age and lack of use, Jim inquired about its history. Learning that it had been a former blacksmith shop and the fact that it was over a hundred years old intrigued him more. Even though it was leaning and dilapidated, he saw something that no one else could see and offered to buy it.

With the deal sealed, he and our teenage son took the logs apart one by one, numbered them and dragged them up the mountain with a four-wheel drive vehicle. He used the timber to build the framework for a cabin; each log had to be reassembled according to the number on it.

Walking up the mountain, they cut trees the size they needed for the roof and the floor and rolled them down to the cabin site. That summer, a one-room cabin with a loft for sleeping was completed.

There were several springs on the property. Choosing one of the larger springs near the top of the mountain, Jim positioned a black rubber pipe into the spring allowing the water to flow down the mountainside. About halfway down, he split the hose adding another line. One permitted fresh spring water to flow into the kitchen sink. The other pipe that split off from the main line carried water to the bathroom. After a septic tank was in place, a modern toilet was installed. Now, we had a place to stay but had no furniture or any necessary items to make it a livable cabin.

Creative Jim went into the nearest town of Burnsville to see what he could find. Wouldn't you know, God sent an old truck loaded with odds and ends and furniture that had seen

Cabin at Burnsville, N.C.

better days. The older gentleman driving the pickup, looking to sell his wares, drove around the town square and low and behold, Jim was there.

It was a lucky day for the driver of the truck. Jim looked over the piled high "junk" and, seeing some useful items, offered to buy it all. The man was happy, and Jim was sure he had made a great deal.

Hearing his vehicle rattle up the mountain, we all went out to see his "find." The smile on his face reflected pure happiness. The rest of us had a look of "are you kidding me"? We found a few useful items and then had to dispose of all the leftovers.

Driving up Kinsey Rd. to our mountain cabin in a four-wheel drive Jeep, was not difficult in Spring and Summer, but winter was a different story. After a snowfall of six to ten inches, the Jeep had to stretch to its limit to get us there. However, walking up, our boots were ankle deep, with every step, in the fresh snow.

After several years of enjoying the mountain top experience, we used it less and less and finally sold it.

Chapter Twenty-Two
The Robbery

Weekends were always busy at the grocery chain where Jim was the store manager. On this particular Friday, customers were bustling up and down the aisles taking advantage of the weekend sales.

Making his way through the back room, he heard over the intercom, "Mr. Kinsey, come to the office". Thinking it wasn't a matter of life and death, he continued his slow pace trying to finish eating an apple as he didn't take time for lunch because the store was so busy. Checking merchandise, as he walked, again he heard, "Mr. Kinsey, come to the office please" Breathing a sigh, thinking he was probably needed to okay a check or speak with a customer, he stepped through the swinging door into the office.

There, he saw two men, one holding an Army 45. "Open the safe!" demanded the one with the gun. Realizing the gravity of the situation, Jim did as he was told without hesitation, but he was praying they wouldn't find a dummy drawer while they rummaged through the office.

The head cashier's face was white with terror. When Jim didn't come the first time she called him, she saw the robbers were getting impatient, and she was fearful they might get rough with her.

With a gun held to Jim's head, the other man scooped up the cash stuffed it in a bag and slipped the bag under his coat. Ordering Jim to come with them, he was told not to make any stupid moves to attract attention.

In the middle of the afternoon, no one noticed anything out of the ordinary as Jim appeared calm, as usual, while walking between two robbers with a gun in his side. Customers were trying to talk to him, but all he could do was smile and keep walking

Outside, they nudged him to walk to the left to the end of the sidewalk where a car was backed in with the motor running. Jim immediately realized that the car probably was the getaway vehicle and he memorized the tag number and the make and model of the car.

When they got to the car, the man with the Army 45 told Jim to turn and face the building. It was at that moment Jim realized he was going to be shot and killed. He stood motionless waiting for the bullet. Thoughts of the children and me were racing through his mind. "What would happen to them"? Thankfully, the men got in the car and drove away.

Rushing back into the store, adrenalin pumping, he called the local police, giving them the details of the robbery along with the description of the car and the tag number. It wasn't until the police cars pulled up to the front of the store with sirens screaming that people realized that something out of the ordinary had occurred. All eyes were on the policemen as they talked to Jim. The policemen drove around the building where Jim had seen the robbers go. However, they found that the robbers had switched cars and got away without a trace. They were never caught.

As Jim relived the moment when he was told to turn and face the building, he remembered that, two weeks before, a manager of another grocery chain, just a few miles down the road, had been killed during a robbery.

He notified his supervisor of the robbery after assessing that the robbers had gotten away with $10,000.00. Jim knew he had to account for that amount of money, but he knew he had followed company policy by making a large bank deposit that morning. Plus, he had also made a dummy drawer where he had another $10,000.00 hidden.

Not wanting me to hear about the robbery, on the news, before he could tell me, Jim had one of the cashiers call me at home to let me know they had been robbed. At first, I couldn't grasp that the store had been held-up, she repeated it. I asked, "robbed?" "What happened?" "Was anybody hurt?" "Is Jim alright?" "Yes," she said, "Mr. Kinsey is alright, he just wants you to come down".

My mind was racing. I could imagine many things. Maybe Jim is hurt, and she didn't want to tell me. I grabbed my purse and car keys. With hands shaking, it took a minute to get the key in the ignition. Driving the three miles to the store, I was trembling and praying for Jim's safety.

When I turned into the parking lot at the store and saw the police car, my knees were weak. Walking nervously into the store and over to the office, the cashier, Jenny, assured me Jim was okay.

Jim saw me and ran over giving me a tight hug. Tears began to trickle down my cheeks, but my heart felt relief, and a secure feeling replaced the fear as he held me in his arms,

This was another time that God had taken care of our family by sparing Jim's life.

Chapter Twenty-Three

Education Journey

With Karyl in high school and Jimmy in middle school, I decided that I was ready to pursue a degree in Education. I enrolled in the community college to start a journey that I had not been able to trek when I was younger.

At the age of forty, married and with two children, my husband took the financial responsibility to allow me to fulfill my dream of earning a college degree.

I enjoyed being in a learning environment and completed the first part of my journey. I didn't know where it would end, but I had earned my Associates in Arts Degree magna cum laude.

Feeling confident with my success at the community college, I continued my education by enrolling in Florida Technological University in Orlando, Florida. With God's help and my family's support, I completed the second part of this journey and received my Bachelor of Arts Degree in Education magna cum laude.

Teaching one year in a local middle school, my thirst for knowledge and the satisfaction of teaching young people, I knew I wanted to study for and earn a master's degree.

After earning my Master's in Education from the University of Central Florida, I chose a teaching career that lasted twenty-eight years. I credit my husband and children for their consistent love and support through this process.

Earned Master's Degree

One summer, I had the opportunity to teach a class for elementary remedial readers at the University of Central Florida.

Proverbs 3:6 says, "In all thy ways acknowledge Him, and He will direct our paths." I know that God has directed my paths. It is evident throughout my life. Without Him in my life, I could not have reached the degree of success that He has allowed me to achieve. I am humbled by His faithfulness to me.

Chapter Twenty-Four
Everyday Life

Both children attended Seminole County Schools from first grade through twelfth. Jim and I were both involved in the children's elementary school as we both were active in the P.T.A. Jim served as treasurer and I was Vice President.

The county school board changed boundaries for school assignments the year that Karyl was a senior, she and Jimmy would now graduate from different schools although living in the same house. After much discussion by the school board, it was decided that seniors already attending a particular school could continue  and graduate from there if they had transportation. Therefore, Karyl graduated from Lake Brantley High School, but Jimmy graduated from Lyman High School three years later.

Jimmy and Karyl on bikes

Karyl's transportation was a 1928 Model A Ford that her dad had bought and refinished inside and out for her one Christmas. It was yellow with black fenders and white leather interior. She named the car Lady Macbeth. Jim kept the original engine in Macbeth because he thought it would be cruel to put a souped-up engine in this classic car.

Lady Macbeth ran great, however, occasionally she would backfire to Karyl's humiliation. One day after school, Karyl was driving Lady Macbeth to her job as a cashier at a supermarket when Macbeth started to jump and bump along. When Karyl heard a hissing sound, she was positive there was a snake in the back seat. Knowing her, I am sure she panicked.

A nice gentleman drove up by her car window and said, "Mam, did you know that you have a flat tire?" With a red face, and after thanking him, she continued to drive, with a flat tire, to the Ford Company that she could see at the corner. She drove Lady Macbeth right onto the Ford lot, got out and called a friend to take her to work.

She called us after she got to work to let us know what had happened

Jimmy and Karyl in the back yard

and asked her dad to please take care of Macbeth. Jim couldn't believe she had left the "Lady" there. When he went to get her, the gate in the back of the Ford company was locked for the weekend. After Karyl graduated and left for college, Lady Macbeth went to another owner.

Leaving for McPherson, Kansas, she enrolled in Central College, a Christian school. She auditioned for the traveling acapella chorus and was accepted as a freshman. Touring through Europe in the summer with the choral group, she said the highlight of the tour was singing in the Cathedral of Notre Dame.

Karyl completed her last two years of study in Orlando, Florida where she graduated with a degree in Respiratory Therapy. She worked as a therapist in hospitals, manager of therapists in a nursing home, and worked in home health care.

She now works as a Corporate Clinical Education Manager with a company that designs and manufactures medical devices for sleep disorders, based in San Diego, California.

Chapter Twenty-Five
Aunt Mary and Uncle Warren

Aunt Mary would say, as she often did, "I don't know what I would do without you, children." Our response to her, every time, was, "What would we have done without you?"

With no children of their own, Aunt Mary and Uncle Warren, unselfishly, were very involved in our lives after mother died. Jenny, Betty, and I spent time with them for various reasons, as needed. Over the years, they were our mentors and supporters. We knew we could count on them for anything.

They never owned a home of their own, probably because they did so much for us. As each of us, three girls, was in high school, Aunt Mary bought our clothes to be sure we were in style.

Uncle Warren preceded her in death. He was in Bel Arbor, our brother Harold's nursing home in Macon, Georgia. Aunt Mary, other family members, and I surrounded his bed the afternoon he was approaching death. I was holding his hand and praying with him when I sensed a light squeeze on my fingers. I felt he let me know he was okay and then he was gone.

After his death, Aunt Mary lived on her own. But throughout the years she was remembered by each of us, and she was never alone on holidays.

At the age of ninety, she was in a nursing home near Jenny in Warner Robbins, Georgia. Jenny, sat with her the night that we had been told her death was imminent. Jenny heard her whispering. Leaning in to listen to what she was saying. She found Aunt Mary was singing in a soft whisper: "Jesus lover of my soul, let me to thy

Karyl and Joe Scott, 2002

bosom fly." What a final testimony!

My other siblings were in Florida attending our daughter's marriage to Joe Scott. Following the wedding ceremony and reception the bride and groom left. The next day, all siblings, nieces, and nephews traveled to Macon, Georgia for Aunt Mary's funeral. Hart's Mortuary handled the arrangements as they had done for other family members through the years. She was buried in Warner Robins, Georgia.

The night Aunt Mary died, I reflected that while one loved one was gone, two loved ones had their lives blended in marriage, and a new beginning.

Romans 6:4 . . . "by the glory of the father, we should walk in newness of life."

Me and Aunt Mary at 90
years old

My Aunt Mary

Christmas is a time to remember those
We love
Your love and care have guided me.
You are like a dove of peace, you see.
You have encouraged and sustained.
You have sacrificed and never complained.
You are more than just an aunt.
You are also mother and friend who helped
 Me advance.
You are not remembered just for material things.
You are remembered for the good-will you bring.
Christmas is a time to remember those
We love.

Written by
Mary Ann Kinsey
Christmas, 1989

Chapter Twenty-Six

Obstacles

Jim, a store manager for a large food chain in Florida, retired early and invested in a plant nursery. He has always found plants calming and relaxing, but a nursery with forty to fifty beds each holding approximately ten thousand floras and another hothouse that housed hundreds of hanging baskets? Karyl and Jimmy both helped out with shipping plants throughout the United States after school each day. Everything was going well; the plant-life was flourishing. Jim was looking forward to the upcoming holiday when they planned to sell hundreds of dish gardens, hanging baskets, and bulk plants. The week before the holiday, Jim went to the nursery to discover that someone had backed a truck up to the locked gate and had cleaned out everything that was ready to sell. Profits dropped to a critical low. This happened three different times. Jim never gives up to adversity, so he put a travel trailer out there and hired someone to live there for security. Plants dwindled slowly, and he finally realized his security guard was running her own business out of there at night.

Still determined to make this business successful, he built it up again. No matter how hard you persevere, natural disasters occur. Hurricane David arrived, and the nursery was flooded threatening the beds that were up off the ground in addition to the hanging baskets. The nursery literally became a lake. We discovered that a neighbor had dammed up his property to keep it from flooding and that had caused the water to back up on our property and flooded the nursery.

Jimmy, a teen, went in the water up to his chest with waders over his jeans to save the hanging baskets. Thankfully, he had his gun. Holding it up above the water, Jimmy saw an alligator swimming toward him. His first thought was to wait for him to get close enough and he would shoot him when he opened his mouth. When the alligator got closer, Jimmy lost his nerve and fired. Missing the gator, it disappeared under the water. Not knowing where the reptile was, Jimmy tried to get out as fast as possible, but a water moccasin slithered by and bit him through his waders. He called Poison Control to ask what to do, and they told him if he was still alive it didn't penetrate his clothes enough to kill him. He did have two small marks from the snakebite, but thankfully it was not deadly.

I attended a meeting with our state representative and showed him pictures of the nursery and explained the situation. He had helicopters and planes fly over the nursery and assess the damage. Eventually, the neighbor was forced to remove the dam from his yard. God was watching over us again.

We have had our share of misfortunes, but Jim, the eternal optimist always says, most millionaires have failed at least seven times before they make it. My response to that was, "I don't want to be a millionaire, and I don't want to fail seven times." That is one example of how we differ, but neither of us had a goal to be a millionaire.

It takes a strong person to keep going with some of the obstacles we have had to overcome, but God always brings us through and makes us stronger. We have so many blessings that the obstacles we have overcome seem very minute.

Chapter Twenty-Seven
"I Can Read! I Can Drive!"

If you could have heard the excitement in a sixth-grade boy's voice when he shouted, "I can read" "I can read," for the first time, you would understand the excitement that I felt as his teacher.

I began my teaching career in a middle school Remedial Reading Lab team teaching with another Reading Specialist. Our teaching philosophy and personalities complimented each other. On a daily basis, our lessons were not divided into neat segments of who would say what when, but we worked together like a well-oiled machine. Words flowed from each of us in a timely manner. Students would look from one to the other of us to see who was speaking.

It was always rewarding to see students improve their reading skills enabling them to advance in their academic classes, but to see a sixth-grade boy change from being a nonreader to realizing he had actually read a portion of a short story was more than rewarding. When he jumped out of his seat saying "I can read! I can read!" I was as excited as he was. Other students stopped to see what the excitement was about. Moments like this enforced my belief in individualized instruction, which usually produced a positive outcome.

An older remedial student who had been retained in earlier grades had low self-esteem. Trying to understand how he felt in classes with younger students, I chose materials that I thought would appeal to his chronological age. Hearing some of the boys talking about wanting to get their driver's license and knowing it would be difficult for them to pass the State Driving Test, I wrote a

Driver's Manuel that they could read; it covered the same materials that were on the state test. Using my Driver's Manual as one of their required resources, I saw the results that I had hoped for when one student came to class one day with a big smile announcing that he had passed the driver's test. The excitement was at a high level. My heart was filled with pride. That boy had higher self-esteem and was now looked up to by other students. The word spread that there was a class that taught Driver's Education. Students who were not in my class came by to see if they could take my Driver's Education Class. They didn't realize that my class was for remedial readers.

Chapter Twenty-Eight
Mary K. and Mary S.

The day I began my teaching career, was a day to remember. My team teacher, Mary S. soon became a valued friend. She was from upstate New York, and I hailed from Georgia. My "southern expressions" completely confused her "northern language." We had a few laughs, and we both got a new education. When talking about someone who couldn't identify a common object, I told Mary S., "He didn't know pea-turkey." "Pea-turkey?" she asked. "What is pea-turkey?" "It is just one of those southern things," I replied. "Never mind, I know, I say some strange things." We both laughed.

Another time, I was driving my daughter's MG convertible on Interstate 4 in Orlando, Florida. A terrible storm was brewing, and the rain started coming down in torrents. The next day, at school, I told Mary S., "While I was driving Karyl's MG convertible with the top down, the rain started, and the bottom fell out!" Horrified, she said, "the bottom fell out of her car?" "No! that is just another one of those southern things." I admitted. "I'll explain later." A few laughs make a merry heart, and there were many laughs over the years.

Friends are usually there for each other, but not all friends will go to the extreme for you. Mary S. and another teacher friend, Fran, have been to the extreme.

One-night Mary S. and Fran saw one of our sixth-grade students at a local Ice Cream Shop in tears. She had wrapped her new retainer in a napkin while she ate her sundae and had left without it. When she returned, it had been thrown away with the garbage.

Trying to calm her, Mary S. said, "Wait here! Mrs. Kinsey has

111

South Seminole Middle School

a metal detector. Fran and I will go get it and will be right back". They drove into our driveway and woke us up to borrow a metal detector! Once awake, we were ready to help out.

In a matter of minutes, Jim and I were dressed and at the Ice Cream Shop plowing through mounds of garbage hoping to hear the beep of the metal detector and reach down and retrieve the retainer. After an hour of moving it, the metal detector up and down and through the garbage, we still had no retainer, but it did beep hundreds of times only to find little foil lids off of the individual coffee creamers.

Saying goodbye to our little sad sixth-grade student and her babysitter, we had ice cream and coffee. Why not? We were already awake.

It was not uncommon to get a phone call at night from Mary S. to go for pie and coffee, so assuming it was her, I picked up the phone. "Hello," I said. "What? Why? Where? Don't hang up!" Click! "Jim, your plant delivery driver just called. Said he was not going to drive anymore and hung up."

"Did he say where the truck was?"

"No, Now what?"

The phone rang again. I rushed to answer hoping it was the driver, but it was Mary wanting us to go for pie.

Telling her no, we couldn't go this time, she heard the stress in my voice and asked if everything was okay? "Actually, no," I replied. and told her our situation.

Not asking but telling me she would come and help us look for the truck that was full of plants, she was there within twenty minutes and had Fran with her. They were game for a scavenger hunt for our delivery truck at ten o'clock at night.

We knew the driver was in the small adjoining town of Apopka and we also knew he could have been in an unsavory place. We drove around Apopka looking in the parking lot of every bar hoping to see our truck. With no luck, we left, and it was the next day that the vehicle was found outside of town.

All our adventures were not late at night but were actually fun and exciting with just the girls. There were several trips on cruise ships to Cancun and the Bahamas and road trips to Canada and Williamsburg, Virginia. There were also many get-a-ways to New Smyrna Beach, Florida.

Teaching was our profession, for a time, but friendships are forever.

Chapter Twenty-Nine

R.T. Reading Time

"I never thought our teachers would let us read for our own enjoyment during class, but I like the idea," Joan said to her friend.

"I like it too, but it would have been fun if Randy Travis had come to our school," her friend replied.

It was our remedial readers in the Reading Lab that sparked the idea to promote pleasure reading during class time. We noticed that when they finished their daily assignments, they went to the bookshelf and selected a book and read. Low-level books were available with titles that boys preferred and titles of interest to girls.

With the support of our principal and faculty, we implemented a school-wide Reading Time that included all faculty, office personnel as well as lunchroom and custodial staff. Students seldom had time to read for pleasure during class, so that was the premise for Reading Time.

Notices were posted around the school campus that simply read, R. T. is Coming. These signs were up four weeks before R. T. was to begin, to create interest. Students were determined to find out what R. T. meant. After not getting any help from teachers or school staff, they decided that R. T. meant that Randy Travis was coming. That idea circulated school until the day R.T. (Reading Time) was announced.

Students were told to select a book that they would like to read, and they were to have it with them at all times as several times during the day. The front office would announce over the intercom that R. T. would begin. At that time, everyone was to take out their book and read for pleasure, for the next five to ten minutes. Teachers, office secretary's lunchroom, and janitorial staff would all stop whatever they were doing and read. Magazines were acceptable only if approved by a teacher.

When students learned that teachers liked to read and were willing to give five or ten minutes of class time to allow them to read anything of their choice they loved the idea. R. T. was announced several times during the day. Students saw Mr. Mossman, their principal and lunchroom ladies reading when R.T. was announced. To see custodians sitting on a wall or step with their push broom laying there, I believe, it made an impact on the importance of reading.

After four weeks of Reading Time, it was time to get back to the usual routine. When students asked for it to continue, my heart beat a happy note. Some students continued carrying a book and read anytime they could catch a minute or two. Not only was R.T. successful, but it was enjoyed.

Chapter Thirty
Multicultural Cookbook

Standing outside my classroom on hall duty, during the first day of new classes, a small sixth-grade girl timidly slithered past me and quickly slid into the first available seat. Looking around hoping to see a familiar face, a smile slowly parted her lips. Then a big smile displayed her braces as she spotted her friend. Now, with more confidence, she moved without hesitation near her friend before class began.

"Around The World in a Tasty Way"

Two macho boys raced through the door together as the tardy bell rang. Looking around, they realized all of the backrow seats were taken. Under his breath, one of them said, "Oh no! We have to sit by girls", as they plopped down in disgust.

Every nine-week period, I gained a different group of students. To ease them into a new situation and a new teacher, I introduced myself and told them something about my family and then I asked each of them to say their name and tell us anything about their family that they would like to share.

After a moment, one boy raised his hand and said, "My name is Sung Ho. I have a big family in Korea. One of my favorite foods is seaweed."

"Yuk," came from across the room. "It is good," said Sung Ho. I called on a boy and learned his name was Walter. I said, "Walter, tell us about your family. If you don't think you would like seaweed, tell us what you do like". He smiled and said he had two sisters and a dog named Rascal. He also said he liked pizza. As each child introduced themselves, many of them included their favorite food. With several students from other countries, a number of unusual foods were mentioned.

Later, when I was alone and thinking out loud, I thought, "Why not put together a multicultural cookbook?" That could include recipes from every student's heritage and would cover many of the English skills I needed to cover in our English curriculum.

Listing skills of spelling, capitals, punctuation, measurements, and interviewing as a few, I was excited about the idea of the students publishing a cookbook, but how would I pay for it?

My principal approved of the project and said that he would cover the cost of publishing it. After thanking him, I left his office so thankful for a principal who supported his teachers and truly put the students first. I couldn't wait to talk to my classes the next day.

When each class came in, I asked them what they thought about compiling a cookbook with their families' recipes. Many of them were immediately interested. Everyone

Me with Mickey Mouse

wanted to talk at once with ideas or questions. "Will it be a real cookbook?" one asked. "Can we put our favorite recipe in it?" said another.

"Yes," I answered.

"What do you think about everyone bringing in a recipe from your heritage or your parents or grandparents heritage? "I asked.

"What does heritage mean?" asked one girl.

"Well, how many of you have someone in your family who came here to America from another country?" I asked.

"Oh, you mean, if my grandparents came here from Italy a long time ago?" a boy interjected.

"It could be a long time ago," I answered.

They all wanted to tell me what their grandparents original country was. Some said theirs came from New York or Texas. I told them we could put a recipe in from anywhere. They agreed that it sounded like fun and they were ready to get started.

Their first assignment was to interview their parent or relative or anyone who took care of them and ask them about their heritage and then to choose a recipe they wanted to put in the cookbook.

The recipe had to be labeled with the name of the country that it represented. Then, they would type it into the computer at school.

They loved that. They knew they would have to go to another classroom to have access to a computer. They would also have to be sure to have correct spelling, punctuation, abbreviations, and measurements. It had to be edited to be sure there were no errors.

After the recipes were collected and entered into the computer, they started planning how to organize them into a cookbook. The students looked at published cookbooks that I had brought to class, to help them to decide where to start. They concluded that they could divide the recipes into sections such as appetizers, meats, desserts, etc.

The students from each class chose the clip art for their recipes and for the country that it represented. In order to select a name for the cookbook, each student in each class could propose their idea for the title. Then, each class would choose the most popular title in their class. With a designated name submitted from each of my five classes, the students voted on those five titles and chose the title, "Around the World In A Tasty Way," for the front cover.

The same process was used to select the best drawing to match the title. All students could submit their sketches for consideration. The illustration voted the best was a grocery bag with a face, legs, and arms full of grocery items clinging onto a country on the globe. Two girls were chosen to write the Introduction.

The county school office printed and collated the pages and furnished the plastic spiral binding. The students inserted the spiral binding into the pages to complete the project of publishing their own cookbook. Each student received their copy.

My assistant principal, Vivian Bowden, encouraged me to enter the student's cookbook into Disney's Teacherrific Competition that was held at Disney World in Orlando, Florida, to recognize Florida teacher's ideas that were done by the students.

After it was entered, my husband and I and my assistant principal were invited to Disney for the celebration of all the entries. It was a very special evening. When all the festivities were over, we all gathered in the amphitheater for the announcement of the winners.

There were several hundred entries, and I was totally surprised when my name was called as a winner for my student's Multicultural Cookbook. I was so shocked, Vivian had to tell me they called my name. I quickly slipped my feet back in my shoes.

My students were the real winners. I was just the one who got to enjoy the festivities and accept the award on their behalf. When I told them that their cookbook had won the Disney Teacherrific Award and that our school had received one thousand dollars, they shouted like they were Olympic Gold Medalists.

I am always pleased when an idea grows to become something that has merit. My teaching technique was successful, in that, all language skills required to be taught by the State of Florida were covered, and my sixth-grade students enjoyed the process and the finished product.

Chapter Thirty-One

1920s

The 1920s and Roaring '20s posters were placed everywhere around our school campus when the students came in on Monday morning. Students bombarded teachers with questions about the meaning of the signs. Students had no idea of what they were going to experience in the next few weeks.

Being one of the two Learning Resource Specialists, in our school, we had gotten permission from our principal to implement a school-wide program around the 1920s theme.

After presenting the idea to the faculty and staff and they joined our enthusiasm, we introduced the concept to

Mary S., principal and me 1920's

the students. With the teachers taking the lead, the students caught on to the excitement and everyone was in for something new.

Teachers in each department had begun planning how their subject content could relate to the 1920s. Examples: Physical Education researched and studied athletes and Olympic medalists of the '20s. Science chose inventors and inventions of the 20s. Home Economics loved 1920s fashions; English selected authors and novels of the 1920s; Math teachers picked math theories and statisticians for that period. Social Studies studied immigrants and Ellis Island.

A room off the media center was set up with antiques of the 1920's

Me and Mary S. in 1920's costumes

and other antiques that were brought in by the faculty, staff and friends. Classes were scheduled to walk through the Antique Room to view and in some cases, handle some of the items.

After studying for several weeks, two days were planned for a final presentation of the Social Studies Department. They had combined all their classes to study and demonstrate the vetting process of immigrants entering America through Ellis Island.

The Media Center was transformed into Ellis Island with several stations set up to demonstrate what it was like when the immigrants first stepped off the boats. Students furnished their own 1920's style clothes. They were carrying their possessions in old suitcases, boxes, and bags. Some carried baby dolls.

The first station was the infirmary to pass health codes. From there, they proceeded to the next station to get immunizations. To process everyone as they went from station-to-station, a lot of waiting took place. As you would imagine, it was much like what the new immigrants experienced. The last station required them to pass an American History Test.

When all immigrants had been through every station, they were sworn in as citizens of the United States Citizens of America. Waving flags, shouting with excitement and throwing hats into the air gave an electrifying feeling of what the early immigrant must have felt.

Every teacher and staff member, including the lunchroom ladies and the janitorial staff, rented 1920's style attire, from a costume store in downtown Orlando, paid for by our principal, with school funds, and everyone wore them throughout the two-day finale. It was gratifying, for me to see the unique Units of Study with the 1920s theme in every discipline. I believe the study was enjoyed by the students as well as the faculty   It was thrilling to see middle school students become so involved with history.

Chapter Thirty-Two
A New Reading Curriculum

The prospect of giving one hundred thirty plus students a chance to improve their reading skills, each nine-week grading period was overwhelming and exciting at the same time.

The English Department Chairman, Cindy Huggins, suggested that we expand the Remedial Reading Lab to include all sixth grade English classes. That way, we could work with all reading levels from remedial through advanced.

We reasoned that if we could get students who were borderline in their reading, we could reach them before they became remedial readers. The advanced readers could only benefit by reinforcing and expanding the skills they already had.

Once the logistics were worked out a new reading curriculum emerged. Each nine-week grading period, one of the sixth-grade English teachers would accompany each of their classes of thirty plus students to the reading lab. The extra pair of hands were needed to keep up with the daily grading when each student completed an assignment. We constantly floated around the room helping those who either needed assistance or had completed their task and was ready to have it graded. Raised hands, sometimes looked like butterflies waving their gossamer wings waiting for one of us to reach them.

At the end of each grading period, Students left with a strong sense of accomplishment and a feeling of self-assurance. All students showed some degree of success. Many average students reached higher levels while the best readers climbed to levels as high as high school.

By scheduling a sixth grade English class each nine-week grading period, we were able to reach all four English teachers and their classes with approximately five hundred twenty plus students.

Nothing could have been more satisfying, to Mary S. and me, than to know that five hundred twenty plus students had the opportunity to raise their reading levels in our classes.

Chapter Thirty-Three
Speech Contest: Look at the Size of that Trophy!

The Tropicana Company sponsored a Speech Contest every year for sixth-grade students in Seminole County Schools.

I announced to the students in my English classes that I would like for them to participate in the contest. I heard groans and "I can't," but after learning that I would walk them through the process step-by-step I had their attention.

I gave them specific guidelines and helped them select a topic. After giving them examples of how to plan and write a speech, they shared their plan with other students who were struggling. It was a joint effort. I often allowed students to share ideas. When they saw another student's thoughts, it often sparked an image for them. I explained the difference in sharing and copying, and that it was not the same as reproducing another's work.

Once their speech was written, they could practice with another student, but they also had to practice it at home. They could use notes to practice and when giving their speech to the class, but could not "read" it.

Everyone was expected to deliver their speech in front of the class and be judged by their classmates and of course by me. I have found that students will usually rule wisely.

Any student who was terrified to stand in front of the class, could meet me during my lunch time and say it in private.

The winner from each of my classes would then give their speech and be judged by several other teachers. The student chosen as best speech and speaker went on to be judged by the judges from the

Tropicana Company along with the winners from the other sixth grade classes.

A student from my class won First Place for our school and then competed with the winner from each of the other middle schools in the county.

I attended the competition along with Mandy's parents and was bursting with pride when she was presented with the First Place Trophy from the Tropicana Company over all sixth-grade in Seminole County schools.

She was so humble when accepting the bigger than life trophy, but when she joined her parents and me later, her comment was, "Where are we going to put this?"

Chapter Thirty-Four
Learning Strategies

"Are we supposed to teach strategies to students in another teacher's class when we are not invited?" I asked my team teacher.

"No teacher would want to be told that a fellow teacher was coming into their classroom and teach their students new strategies without their consent," Mary confirmed.

The Board of Education integrated a new Learning Strategies Curriculum in all middle schools in our county. The new curriculum was presented to my former team teacher and me. We were both interested in working together again.

After teaching sixth-grade English for three years, I accepted the position along with Mary S. But we would enter another teacher's domain only if they invited us into their classrooms.

Teachers were gracious and wanted to have the new curriculum available to them. When they learned that they could ask us to teach their students with the innovative strategies to fit their lesson, they were "in." We were ready to plan for any subject area that was needed.

Teachers would give us the lesson they wanted to teach. We would go back to our office and plan one or more strategies to fit.

The teacher was always in the classroom while the lesson was taught. They could see if the students grasped the concepts they wanted them to understand and possibly see a new approach as a way to solve a problem.

Our teachers were open and willing for us to come into their classroom and work with their students offering new strategies and ideas.

The curriculum was successful and was being used every day for three years before it was eliminated by the Board of Education.

I was disappointed. It appears, that when a program reaches a level of success, funds are cut and so is the plan.

I moved again to work with seventh-grade remedial readers while my friend went back to a sixth-grade remedial class.

Chapter Thirty-Five
Poetry Alive

How can a poem be alive one might ask? I say, "You'll see."

Joining my students with the students from Randy Allman's gifted classes was not unusual for us, as we both had the same philosophy and similar styles of teaching.

Performing poetry can make it come alive; I told my students. Both classes were given the same guidelines for our unit on poetry.

They could select any poem of their choice to memorize, and they could decide how they could perform it. They would not be judged on the length nor the difficulty of the poem they chose. They would only be judged on the creativity and the performance itself.

To give them examples of what we expected, both of us performed a poem of our choice. I chose "Merry-Go-Round" to demonstrate 'round and round' and 'up and down.' Mr. Allman was six feet tall, so it was not surprising that he wanted a poem about basketball.

They had a week to make their selection and practice the way they would perform it. They had access to poetry in our classrooms, in the media center and could use any that they might have at home. The students had class time to scour through books looking for just the right poem.

The following week, Mr. Allman and I had scheduled our classes in the media center so that we could have them together for their performances.

I believe that they read more poetry this way than if we had assigned a specific poem for them to look at and perform. That would have been more difficult than making their own choice.

I remember specifically the Shel Silverstein poem, "Boa Con-strictor" performed by a boy in my class. It was hilarious. On a more serious note, a girl from the gifted class performed "The Highwayman" by Alfred Noyes.

My average students did as well as the gifted students. It was a way to teach poetry without intimidation.

Chapter Thirty-Six
A New Idea

"A Foxfire magazine lay open on my desk. Would that really work?" I mused. I was intrigued by the unorthodox method of teaching that was used by an English teacher in a school in North Georgia.

I was teaching sixth-grade English at the time, and I agreed that students learn best when they are engaged in meaningful activities. Letting students choose how they wanted to learn was a new idea to me, but I decided to use this new pedagogy in my classroom.

I wanted learning to be relevant to my students, but it was difficult for me to relinquish my authority and control in deciding what they wanted to learn.

Each class made their decision on how they would study for the next unit. I was pleasantly surprised at the maturity of each class and how responsible they were.

One class chose to write a play and perform it for another class. Another project of study was to produce an Art Mural relevant to education. Writing to state legislators about their concerns of the educational system was decided by a class. Another class made videos.

My classroom could have appeared chaotic to some as every class period the desks had to be rearranged according to the activity for that class.

To see the enthusiasm and respect the students had for each other was rewarding to me.

I have always believed that learning should and can be fun as long as order was maintained, and the skills required were met.

Was it worth giving my students freedom to learn in a different way? Yes! One might think that I was relaxed and not involved throughout this whole process. That would be a wrong assumption! It was physically exhausting for me. Rearranging desks each class period and keeping order while students were waiting for their turn to speak or crawl around on the floor drawing on their section of a six-foot mural was a busy time. I was totally involved.

I was just as proud of their accomplishments as they were. I could see the pride on their faces and how they carried themselves especially when other students asked them about how they liked their class.

This new method worked well, and the students responded with enthusiasm.

Chapter Thirty-Seven

Creative Writing: Bag Lady

It is difficult for students to know how to begin writing a story. Choosing a topic can be the hardest. Without some guidance, students might sit the entire class waiting for some magic to happen. Understanding their dilemma, I decided to help them with a different approach.

One day, I walked into my classroom dressed like a bag lady, pulling a little red wagon loaded with a large black trash bag filled with a variety of clothing items.

Student's weren't sure how to react. Some laughed, but others just stared with mouths open in disbelief. Taking a few minutes for them to regain their composure, I explained that there were different articles of clothing in the black bag and each one of them was going to reach into it and pull out one item without looking. Whatever they pulled out was the topic of their story. They could write anything they wanted to as long as they included the article they had gotten.

Some pulled out an old shoe, a lady's belt, a straw hat, or something wearable. There were lots of giggles, but some became very serious. One boy had gotten a little dress coat that my son had worn when he was two. His story was one of the most unique from his class. He wrote in first-person that he was a stockbroker on Wall Street. Some stories were humorous, and some were sad.

After the first class, the word spread about Mrs. Kinsey's red wagon and the bag of clothes. Even the Assistant Principal stopped by to watch a class's reaction to the items they pulled from it. Overall it was a great experience.

I enjoyed reading every story and each one reinforced to me that students will produce if they are not intimidated. It was a fun assignment for the students, and I enjoyed performing a little bit myself.

Chapter Thirty-Eight
Reading In Science
Another New Opportunity!

One year an eighth grade Science teacher approached my colleague and me about considering a science curriculum to teach reading skills to her eighth graders who were struggling with the science vocabulary.

After discussing this idea, we decided that I would take these students and work with them and Mary would continue in the sixth-grade Reading Lab. That was when I started teaching reading in the science content area. To prepare for this new challenge, I read the eighth-grade science textbook to see the most important words needed to understand the content. I developed a Science Vocabulary Test that would give me an indication of where to begin with each student.

Their teacher accompanied her low-level group of students to my classroom. Each student was tested and placed in an individualized program for a nine-week period. The students became engaged in the variety of materials that I chose for them.

At the end of the nine-week period, each student was retested to determine what gains, if any, had been made. Some students made more of a gain than others, but all did show some success when I compared their exit score to the entry score.

At the end of the nine-week period, each student was given a written evaluation sheet to get their opinion on the effectiveness of the program and whether they would recommend it to their friends.

Every student indicated that they would recommend this program to their friends. That meant success, to me, and it gave me a feeling of satisfaction.

Chapter Thirty-Nine
Five Ladies in a Station Wagon

I had never been to Mexico, but the more I thought about it, the more I wanted to go. But I'm a mother. "That would be selfish," I thought. "Yet again, it would be a great experience," I decided.

After the children had gone to bed, I began talking about Mexico with my husband. Finally, he asked, "What is this about Mexico"?

"Well", I explained the whole deal. My Spanish professor had invited me to go with her and three other ladies to Mexico. The trip was just months away. I was feeling guilty, but Jim said, "You should go."

I told Karyl and Jimmy about the trip and that I had talked to our friends who graciously volunteered to keep them while Jim was working. Karyl and Jimmy got excited to stay with their friends, Mark and Marie. I started planning, and when I thought about the expense, I questioned whether I should be spending money on this.

We had a few acres outside of town where my husband had a small plant nursery and a few heads of cattle and several pigs. Knowing that I was feeling guilty about money, he offered to plant some extra caladiums for me so that when they were ready to sell, he would give me the profit for my trip. That sounded like a good idea. Feeling like I should help out, every day after my Spanish class, I would drive out to the nursery to see how they were growing. Every time I went by to see them (that was my help), they looked like they were growing fine.

In a few weeks, they were ready to sell. They were healthy with beautiful bold colors. The leaves were large and sturdy. Stopping by the day before he was to take them to market, I walked over to the rows where the caladiums had been planted; there was nothing there. There were only bits of roots visible in the bright sunlight.

"What happened," I yelled. "Jim, what happened"? Coming around the corner of the hothouse, he said, "Sorry, the cows got out and had a very expensive lunch."

"Oh no, my poor caladiums," I moaned. "My trip, oh no," I whispered. Poor Jim felt awful. Somehow, I knew I would still go on this trip.

Sometimes time heals, so, as planned, we left Orlando early one morning, with all five ladies settled in the brown and gold station wagon waving good-by to our families promising to bring gifts back to everybody.

Three of us were settled in the back seat with me in the center. After a couple of hours into the trip and talking about some of the things and places we were going to see, I was beginning to feel my tired body relaxing. Changing seat positions gave me a seat by the door where I could rest my head on the window frame. Everyone had their chance to sit in the middle except the driver of course.

That first day, driving to New Orleans on Interstate 10 we had to drive through Biloxi, Mississippi and were shocked at the devastation that Hurricane Camille had left behind the year earlier.

Arriving in New Orleans, in the late afternoon, and after checking in to our hotel, we walked down Bourbon St. to Preservation Hall to listen to Jazz musicians play improvisations until we decided that we should go back to the hotel as we had another long day in about six hours.

Up early the next morning, we drove to Brownsville, Texas on the

Mexican border. Despite the fact that we were tired from a long day, we took a short walk around the grounds of the resort until a group of young men found our young, single Spanish Professor attractive. Amid wolf whistles and comments in Spanish, we thought it best to return to our rooms for the night. Settling in for the evening, I had some time to call Jim and fill him in on how the trip was going and to check in on the children.

Crossing the border, the next morning, we drove to a little border town for lunch. After parking on the narrow street, two small boys asked if they could watch our car. Realizing that they wanted payment for their service, we offered five pesos which they accepted with wide smiles.

Practicing my Spanish, I ordered a lunch of fried tortillas and fish soup that had a very strong fish taste. I discovered that the lime served on the dish was there for a purpose. Squeezing the lime juice into the soup, gave it a smooth, delicate taste. Our little guards took their job of watching our car seriously. From the restaurant window, we saw them walking around it and wiping the front end with an old cloth.

Driving another long day, as we went over the crest of a hill, the lights of Mexico City illuminated the sky. Oohs and aahs escaped the lips of those of us who were surprised at the size of the city. We unloaded our luggage to enter the hotel, which we discovered was unusual for five women to be alone at night as men were normally the ones out while the women remained at home.

The beautiful hotel with its efficient staff didn't keep these gringos from getting sick from the water. Four of the five were not feeling well enough to leave the hotel. So, as I was the only one who was not ill, I was chosen to find a Pharmacia and use my limited Spanish to bring back a miracle drug so that we could get on with our adventure. I actually got the pharmacist to understand what I wanted and returned with the medicine that got the sick up and walking again.

Using taxi cabs to get around the city was terrifying, to me, as there were no marked lanes on the streets. The taxi drivers never applied their brakes, but just sat on their car horns and kept moving in and out of heavy traffic. It was less stressful just to keep my eyes closed.

Our first stop, today, was to walk around the Floating Gardens of Xochimilco. The boats were loaded with every kind of flower indigenous to the area. We could not resist purchasing a large bouquet to take back to our hotel room. The vibrant colors and the fresh aroma were pleasant to wake up to in the mornings.

After some shopping and attending a Bull Fight, we were ready to make our way south to see the pyramids of Teotihuacan and down to the city of Pueblo where we could see the Volcano Popocatepetl

The silver mines in the town of Taxco were what had lured us that far south. Shopping in the open storefronts and walking on cobblestone streets was part of the quaint atmosphere of years past. Tourists and native Mexicans crowded the shopping district.

With my arms filled with treasures, hurrying to catch up with my friends, a young boy joined my stride while holding up his arm that was filled with cheap glass beads. Taking one strand of the beads, and holding them close to my face, he asked "Cinco pesos?" Without looking at them, I replied, "No, gracious." Not giving up, he held them high and asked again "Quatro pesos?" I said "No."

Finally, he lowered the price and with exasperation asked, "Uno pesos?" Facing him, I said "No." Giving me a dirty look, he said in perfect English, "Forget it, lady," and he ran away looking for another gringo who might buy his beads.

Oaxaca was the most southern and the most beautiful places that we visited. We stayed our last night in a cottage near what had been, at one time, the Governor's mansion.

As we started our return trip home, we were high in the mountains on a narrow road with no guard rails. We had driven for hours without seeing another human, not even another car. Rounding a sharp curve on the edge of a precipice, we felt a bump, bump. "Oh no," I thought. "Is it really a flat tire?" We all got out to survey the situation. Yes, it was a flat tire. I knew nothing about changing a tire. I hoped someone knew. The only thing to do was to unload the back end of the station wagon to get to the spare tire. We all started removing the luggage along with all of the souvenirs and paraphernalia we had collected along the way.

As we were unloading, a service truck appeared out of nowhere. Two Mexican men jumped out of the cab, changed the tire, refused payment, drove off, and we never saw them again.

Some would say that we were lucky, but I believe in miracles. That service truck, with two angels, was sent from heaven. It disappeared as quickly as it had appeared.

Days later, when we reached the Mexican - U. S. Border, all of the purchases that we, five ladies, had accumulated must have overwhelmed the Border Patrol. He looked in the back of the station wagon, and he evidently thought we looked harmless or he really didn't want to go through all of that stuff, so he just waved us through.

When we got back to Florida, we had gifts for family and friends as we had promised.

Chapter Forty
Teacher Exchange Program

I was privileged to observe the similarities and differences in the educational system of England and the United States; it was an honor and very enlightening.

Finally arriving in Grimsby, a large town and seaport in Lincolnshire, I met my hosts Mark and Allison. Going for a lunch of fish and chips, I was introduced to being served my first whole fish with head included. The eyes seemed particularly large, but I managed to eat it graciously.

After lunch, I was able to shop in a bookstore and purchased a book on tales of the North Sea.

Getting settled in the home of my hosts, I was surprised that the nights in the summer are very short. It was as light at midnight as it was in the afternoon.

Mark was a middle-school teacher and was on the testing committee in Humber County. He had a meeting to evaluate and plan

Me with Children in Grimsby, England

their testing content and procedures; I was invited to go with him. I enjoyed riding over the hills and through the valleys of the beautiful countryside with the blooming wildflowers that covered acres with a diversity of colors. I was able to join Mark in the meeting and learned a smidgen of how they determined their requirements and procedures of testing.

I was invited to visit all levels of schools from pre-school through College. Speaking to a group of Primary School children, approximately first through third-grade, I had been asked to talk to them about American schools and what life was like for children in America. During a question and answer period, one little boy, about seven, asked if I lived near Zimbabwe. I explained that Zimbabwe was a long way from where I lived but that I did live near Disney World. I knew most of them had heard of Disney World and after that many questions about Disney were asked. They were so engaged that the principal extended my time with them. I believe that one of the reasons they enjoyed the question and answer time was that they wanted to hear my American accent. Needless to say, I enjoyed listening to their British accent, as well, and that was one of my favorite stopovers.

When visiting one of the colleges, I was surprised that when the students had a break, they went outside with their professors, sat on a grassy knoll, and had wine and cheese. I didn't get to observe a class, but I did get to see the beautiful campus.

I was accustomed to colorful, interesting classrooms and was surprised when Mark collected a classroom set of books from a closet before entering the class. Passing the books out to each of the students, he had them take turns reading round-robin. I was used to more engaged activities, but they were very attentive and excited just to define words that Mark read from a list.

I learned that truant students were not really a big concern as they were thought of as troublemakers and the classes were better off without their interruptions.

One thing that I found most troubling was that students were categorized by eighth-grade as to whether they should continue their education or find work as an apprentice and learn a trade.

My hosts were very gracious and included me in several social events of their friends. I had many warm Coca Colas served with a slice of lemon.

All of my time in England was not in school settings. I had time to see some of the places of interest.

I visited one of the fishing boats that was docked on the Humber Estuary near where it reaches the North Sea. The smell of the oil from the engine room permeated the entire vessel. Walking through the sleeping quarters, I was surprised at the small space with bunk beds built three deep. Everything was thick with oil, grim and sea salt, but the young men were busy preparing to go back out on the North Sea the next day.

It told a story of a rough life for the young men who would be at sea for long periods of time away from family. Many of them would stay with a boat until they were old, only experiencing life on a fishing boat.

Could these young men have been discouraged from continuing their education in exchange for living a life of hard, relentless work fighting the elements, for a lifetime, on a fishing boat?

While in Lincolnshire, I visited the Lincoln Cathedral with

gothic architecture that was built in 1072. It was difficult to imagine a structure that old with such beauty. The stained-glass windows sent dazzling colors caused by the sunlight blinking in and out. The most amazing thing, to me, was that famous women were buried in large concrete, above ground, graves inside the cathedral.

Mark's friends invited him to bring me to London so that I could see the city and enjoy the sites. St. Paul's Cathedral and Westminster Abby along with Big Ben and the Houses of Parliament were part of my walking tour the first day. Being able to see the Tower Bridge and the Tower of London were special, but seeing the Crown Jewels, I was overcome with wonder at the magnitude and beauty of them.

Strolling through Covent Garden enjoying street performers and eating a hamburger, we, then, rode the tube, got off and walked to Buckingham Palace to see the changing of the guards.

Returning to Grimsby, I picked up last minute gifts, and it was time to return home to America. The three weeks spent in England was a wonderful experience. I was anxious to return to my school and share what I had observed about the differences in philosophy in education in England versus the United States.

I was more focused on strengthening our educational philosophy, making sure that we use every possible means to ensure that every student would be encouraged to continue their education after they left middle school and continued to high school. We recognize that not all students are mature enough to appreciate their schooling until after they reach the higher grades. Late bloomers, as we call them, sometimes go on to become leaders in the community. I wondered, "What if" they were not given the opportunity to grow.

Later, Mark came to America to visit our schools in Florida and lived with Jim and me. After meeting him in downtown Orlando, I stopped by the groomer to pick up our little white Bichon Frise, Princess. I knew that Mark was not fond of dogs, but Princess was special. We had acquired her from the very spoiled Princess of Saudi Arabia. A doorman at the hotel told Jim that the Princess had grown tired of the little white dog and would give her away. Within the week, Jim brought her home.

Princess decided that Mark needed her love and she stayed close to him at all times. By the time he left to return to England, he was taking pictures of her to show off to his friends in Grimsby.

He went to several county meetings, with me, where he was able to sit in on several sessions with a topic that was of interest to him. He observed different strategies that were used to reach the students.

He also spent time in my classroom where he saw students in groups, using machines for their individual programs while others were working independently. Sharing ideas and philosophies is a great way for all of us to grow.

The Orlando area in Florida has much to offer in entertainment. We spent a long day at Disney World taking in as many attractions as possible. It was probably equal to three normal days of sightseeing.

The alligator farms are usually a big attraction where men wrestle with alligators and tourists, brave enough, can feed them. Mark decided not to risk losing a hand.

Taking Mark to his first American baseball game was the ultimate dream for him. It was a beautiful night in the stands eating the all American hot dog with a really cold Coca Cola.

Going to an Arena Football game that was played inside, was a new adventure, but he was more amazed that there were groups of girls out together at a sports event without a date. It appeared that he saw the girls as strong.

Mark attended several social events with my friends and colleagues, but the thing I think Mark enjoyed most was driving my Ford Mustang. He had a Volkswagen back in England, as many people did, with gasoline prices over four dollars a gallon. In the evenings he enjoyed taking the Mustang down to the Pizza Parlor, not far from our house, for a calzone and to talk with other Americans.

It was a pleasure having him in our home as he and Jim had many conversations about American History and politics. It was quite an experience for all of us.

Chapter Forty-One
Adversity Conquered by Faith and Perseverance

My great niece, Kimberly Renee, was born with complete congenital arhinia which was the complete absence of a nose at birth and choanal atresia is the total blockage of the back of the nasal passage. Kallmann syndrome is having the lack of puberty hormones and the inability to smell. Coloboma iris is the result of the "keyhole" appearance of the pupil that causes light sensitivities and sight limitations.

When the doctors at the Army Hospital in Germany, where she was born, saw the situation they faced, they quickly decided to drill a hole through her face to create a small passage for her to breathe. Their quick action and expert placement for the nasal passage proved to have been a perfect placement. With that complete, a tiny plastic tube was inserted into the opening leaving one-half inch of it protruding outside on her little face. A small gold safety pin held the hose in place, keeping it from falling through the opening into her throat and choking her.

Kim was an adorable, beautiful little girl with big blue eyes and blond curls. As she grew, people watched her bounce along with her mother holding her hand, and they often complimented her about her clothes.

When Kim turned around to face the voice that she had

Kimberly at 6 months

heard, faces tried to cover their shock. Many were very kind and would continue to talk to her. This kind of thing happened often. Kim was a happy child and handled similar incidences with a grace that many adults could not.

Kimberly at 7 Years Old

When Kim was two years old, she visited us from Michigan. Our neighbor and family dentist, Ernest Harris, was amazed at her personality and wanted to do something to change the little gold safety pin. Even though it was functional, it was not attractive, so Dr. Harris made a small platinum hoop to replace the fastener. It was a much-needed improvement and was greatly appreciated by all the family.

As Kim approached kindergarten age, her pediatrician in Michigan made a mold of his own four-year-old daughter's nose and created an artificial nose for Kim. It had to be attached to her face, over the tube, with a type of glue every morning before she left for kindergarten.

One day at school, it fell off, but Kim told the children, "I was born this way, and it doesn't hurt at all." That seemed to satisfy everyone. The teacher was amazed at her response and her attitude.

Later, another small nose was made for her of flesh and bone. It was not a prosthetic. It was permanently grafted to her face which allowed her to breathe through her nose.

From eight through ten years of age, she missed most of the school year due to fourteen facial plastic surgeries to produce a small basic nose. She now had a nose that fit the face of a 90-lb.

middle-schooler. As she grew into adulthood, it became evident that this nose was lacking in many ways and eventually she lost the ability to breathe through it. She sounded very nasally, and sinus infections were frequent.

As she grew, the nose did not. Therefore, she went to high school and college with a very small nose. There were many cruel remarks, stares and I assume, there were few close friends. If she ever had lonely days, she never complained or indulged in self-pity.

She had a strong personality and worked her way through college, She and three other girls shared a house near Florida Southern College. She achieved her goal of getting a degree in Social Work.

Employed as a social worker at a Central Florida Hospital she continued to face adversity. One day, a doctor said, in her presence, that he didn't know they had a high-functioning Down Syndrome working here. The nurses were quick to defend her and let him know as if he couldn't figure it out, that she had a birth-defect. It is hard to imagine the hurt that remark inflected on her. Her friends and colleagues were very supportive and encouraged her.

Continuing to work with her highest intensity and integrity, she was named "Employee of the Year" at the same hospital. I can only imagine that the recognition from her colleagues was very special to her. I am so proud of her.

She met a wonderful young man through her future mother-in-law. She and Eric were married and later adopted a bi-racial baby girl when she was only four days old. She was named Erica for her dad, Eric. She is a blessing to the entire family.

Kimberly learned of a surgeon in Tampa, Florida who she thought might be able to do the reconstructive surgery. She had hoped and prayed for just such a physician. She made an appointment with him, and she and her husband went to his office to find a waiting room with many people waiting to see the same doctor.

The doctor called them into his office and began asking them questions about their life in general. He was amazed at her story and how she had been able to earn a college degree, worked as a social worker, married and had adopted a child.

He could visibly see the small nose on her face and, I feel, that he imagined the hurtful life that she had endured. He also saw what a strong person with a will to persevere and conquer adversity.

Taking Kim as his patient was one of the most exciting journeys she would travel. The surgery was done over five years. He began inside with tiny steps preparing for each following step. He had to open the nasal passage again as it had closed up years before leaving her only to be able to breathe through her mouth. She was willing to suffer through eight surgeries to reach the final goal.

One final surgery! The perfect nose made to compliment the size of her face and her complexion was finally in place. It took several weeks for the swelling to go down, but Kim knew it was a small price to pay to achieve the goal she had always desired.

If you could see her today, you would never know the adversity she had endured nor her perseverance to conquer it. She is an amazing young woman.

God answered our prayers again, just as he did with each improvement that she received along the way. This surgery was the ultimate. Thanks to this doctor with his knowledge, skill, and the desire to change her life.

One day, while working at the hospital Kim had to visit a patient to talk about moving her to hospice. That could have been a time when that very sick lady would have been thinking about herself, but she looked at Kim and said kindly, "You have had surgery, haven't you?"

"Yes," Kim answered. The lady responded with, "You look beautiful!"

Kim said she was so overwhelmed with appreciation and love for this lady

Kimberly today, as an adult

that she stayed, talked, and prayed with her. What a wonderful moment for Kim and her new friend. This kind lady passed away, but she will never be forgotten by Kim. What a precious memory.

Chapter Forty-Two

Opportunities

I believe that God has put people in my life for a specific purpose. Several of them come to mind, and I am thankful that they became a part of my life.

A teenage boy left Jim's store without paying for a magazine, but when he was approached, he admitted it and knew it was wrong. Continuing to talk to him, Jim learned that his mother, a former customer, had died recently and he had no place to live. He had been sneaking into the house, through a window, to sleep at night.

Jim wanted to know more about him, so to see if he was sincere about stealing and his story he asked him if he would like to go church with us. When the agreed time came, he was there waiting just as he had said. Jim offered him a job, which he quickly accepted. After working a few days, Jim saw that he was dependable and grateful to have the job.

One afternoon, Jim called me, from the store, and asked me what I thought about letting this boy live with us for a while. I agreed, and he arrived with a load of dirty laundry and a shy smile.

Our children were thrilled and told their friends that their big brother had come home from college. The next thing I knew, all the kids in the neighborhood had come to see their big brother.

After living with us for a while, he saw that God was a normal part of our lives. When he came back to work from lunch, one day, he had walked over to the Bible Book Store and bought Jim a Bible. He was very polite and appreciative of the job and a place to stay. Jim still has the Bible and has fond memories of the young boy who gave it to him.

He lived with us for four months until we found him an apartment and got him settled.

We learned years later that he was a police officer with the local police department. We were thankful for his success.

* * *

Most teenagers are anxious to learn to drive. But to one teenage girl, attending our church, learning to drive was a necessity as her father was dying in a hospital miles away and her mother and siblings wanted to visit him.

The mother was a very frail lady who had never driven. There were three children younger than this young girl. Knowing they had a car but there was no one to operate it, I decided that this family was desperate to see their father and I wanted to do something. I took her out on Sunday afternoons to practice driving. It only took a few afternoons for her to learn. She got her license, and the family was able to visit their father several times before he died.

That young girl, later, became Head of the Mathematics Department in the county school office.

Would either of these young people have been successful without my help? Absolutely! I feel that when God gives me an opportunity to help if I can, it is up to me to respond.

* * *

A student in one of my classes had a very negative attitude and outlook on life. I talked with him many times trying to encourage him, without much success. I was so concerned that I finally asked him if he ever went to church, hoping maybe there was someone who might be able to reach him. Nothing seemed to work, so I told him that Jesus was the only one that I knew that could help him. He said that nothing good had ever happened to him, so he thought he would just walk in front of a car and end it all. I reasoned with him that he might not die and could be an invalid the rest of his life.

Desperate to help him, I asked my husband to give him a job thinking that it might give him some degree of hope. Jim did give him a job, but he wasn't able to stay focused on the simplest of tasks. After several weeks of working with him, Jim realized that he just couldn't do the job and had to let him go.

Several years later, I was pleased to see him with a wife and a child, but sadly, not long after that, I heard that he was hit and killed by a car as he walked along a two-lane road.

Remembering what he had told me when he was in sixth-grade, I will always wonder if his death was an accident or planned. It saddened me, but I knew that I had accepted the opportunity that God had given me regardless of the outcome. I will always remember Donald.

Chapter Forty-Three

Retirement Party

When three teachers retire the same year, it calls for a party. That is just what our faculty and staff planned for Carole Rohr, Diane Rafferty, and me.

Some of the personnel sang an original song to those of us who had survived physical injuries while teaching. It was written by Mary Schiano, and sung to the tune of "Surrey with The Fringe On Top."

There were funny memories told by some of our colleagues. Some others offered words of hope like "Take us with you." It was a very festive time, but there were also times of sadness when we thought about the finality of leaving friends to begin anew in another place and another time of our lives. Each of us received a special gift from their department.

Before the last hoorah, Carole, Diane and I sang a Retirement Song written for us by Mary Schiano, to sing to those we were leaving behind. The lyrics were sung to the tune of "Wouldn't It Be Loverly?"

Diane, Carol and me

Every teacher should be fortunate enough to teach in a school with so much support and respect as I had.

RETIREMENT SONG - SSMS
Sung by Diane, Carole and Mary Ann
May 31, 2001
To - "Wouldn't It Be Loverly"

1. All we want as we leave from here

   Is to wish you a great next year.

   You said you'd stay in touch. Oh wouldn't that be loverly.

2. Thirty years full of memories

   In our hearts is the place they'll be.

   You said you'd stay in touch. Oh wouldn't that be loverly.

     - No more setting the clock and getting up at 5 or 6.

        We look forward for the chance to spend the day as we wish

3. But my friends we will always be

   Part of this special family

   You said you'd stay in touch. Oh wouldn't that be loverly

     - No more setting the clock and getting up at 5 or 6
       We look forward for the chance to spend the day as we
wish

Repeat Verse 3

   But my friends we will always be
   Part of this special family
   You said you'd stay in touch. Oh would-n"t - that-
   Be loverly, loverly, loverly, loverly

(Written by Mary Schiano

Chapter Forty-Four

Surprise!

Another Retirement Party! My daughter, Karyl, surprised me by having many of my family members, longtime friends, and my faculty celebrate with me again.

My friends, Mary, and Fran, helped Karyl keep the surprise by having me plan to go with them to a Baby Shower for one of our friends.

With a baby gift in hand, I walked into the Longwood Community Building expecting to see baby decorations.

What a surprise! One hundred plus friends and family stood and shouted "Surprise!" Jim was smiling like he was so proud of himself for not giving away the surprise.

I was excited to see the attendants from my wedding. We had kept in touch over the forty-seven years since the wedding, but to see them all at my retirement party was special.

I introduced my family who had come from Warner Robins, Georgia, and everywhere in between to Orlando, Florida.

The party theme was in keeping with my teaching career. Each table had a set of three out of print books topped with a little red schoolhouse showcasing my school's colors of red with white lettering of S.S.M.S. for South Seminole Middle School.

A table filled with memorabilia from my life included a doll crafted in my likeness that had been designed from a picture of me as a child. Made by a doll maker in Cocoa Beach, Florida. Every guest received a special bookmark created by Karyl. I received many kudos from my friends that day.

The food that Karyl prepared and served with the help of two of her friends was outstanding.

Karyl is talented and creative, as this party exemplified. Every mom should be so blessed.

Chapter Forty-Five

Retirement

I retired from teaching after twenty-eight years, of working with middle school students from remedial to advanced readers. I taught sixth-grade English before working with teachers in all subject areas as one of the two Learning Resource Specialists to demonstrate Learning Strategies to students at all grade levels.

Those days left indelible memories from the joy of seeing a child's excitement when he realized he had read something for the first time. To the sad day when a parent, whom I had never met, called me at school and asked me if I would adopt their precious little sixth-grade girl. Joy and heartache come with the job.

The day after my retirement, my husband and I moved to Otto, North Carolina in June of 2001. Five of my colleagues drove to the mountains with me for a few days to exchange stories and celebrate life and retirement. Diane and I arrived the day after school was out, while Carole and Cindy came next to be greeted by Diane, Jim and me at Mountain Laurel Cove. Fran and Mary arrived on Saturday bringing fun and laughter.

Some of our time was spent telling stories and singing songs by a campfire with Mary on the guitar. We enjoyed a night at Pickin on the Square, eating at the Dillard House and the Gazebo. We visited the Fox Fire Museum, but

Carole, Cindy, Diane & husband, John, Fran and Mary S. on guitar

the best memory was sitting on my upstairs porch drinking a cup of coffee every morning.

We worshipped together on Sunday - one God. Teaching together for twenty eight years bound us into a priceless friendship. Carole and Cindy returned every summer for thirteen summers. Mary and Fran have returned many times throughout the years to either celebrate our birthdays, Christmas or any number of special occasions. Diane and her husband bought a fifth wheel to travel the western U.S.

We had bought a house on five acres earlier and were looking

Mary S., me, Carol and Diane

forward to living with the view of the Fish Hawk mountain range in Macon County.

Arriving in the early afternoon, when we turned onto the property, the blooming Mountain Laurel hung like a canopy over the driveway. It gave the illusion of driving through a cloud of pink. On the West side of the house, each bloom on the tall Rhododendron bush resembled an artist's painting done with a delicate stroke of lavender.

It was an exciting time, but we were leaving the "known" and facing the "unknown" when we left family and friends of a lifetime.

Settling into a normal life of attending church, joining the Christian Women's Connection proved to be a valuable asset for me, I was able to connect with other women and at the same time, strengthen my faith.

Living in North Carolina for three short months, on our way back to Florida for a visit, we stopped at a local market to pick up a few gifts for friends. As we walked into the market, the atmosphere was somber. Customers were motionless, staring in disbelief as they watched the news on the TV hanging on the wall. The Twin Towers had been attacked with planes by terrorists killing thousands of Americans. There was a heavy feeling in the air. After taking a few minutes to absorb the nightmarish news, with an unprecedented sadness, we continued our drive south.

The air was eerily quiet with no planes flying overhead. President Bush had ordered all planes grounded. We could not escape the deadly silence in the air as we drove near the Atlanta airport, nor the disbelief of this attack on America. Our world, as we knew it, had changed instantly. We as Americans vowed never to forget. Every September 11th, we are reminded of the terror attack on American soil. WE WILL NOT FORGET!

Chapter Forty-Six

Hurricane Katrina Changed Our Lives In North Carolina

The local television station broke in the regularly scheduled program with an update on Hurricane Katrina as it fast approached the Mississippi Coast. For days residents had listened intently to its threat remembering the devastation of Hurricane Camille in 1969 vividly.

The news reporter continued to remind everyone to prepare to protect their property by collecting food and medical supplies, checking vehicles for gas and tire safety; if evacuation is necessary. If mandatory evacuations are issued, please evacuate immediately. Keep your family in a positive attitude with a plan to stay together or in the worst-case scenario, if anyone is separated, plan ways to protect themselves. The most important thing to remember is to remain calm and wait for help.

Katrina, now a category four hurricane, has been packing winds up to 100 mph for the last 24 hours. Our son, Jimmy, wife, Lori, and children, Kyle, Destiny, Levi, and Devon secured their home in Biloxi (as much as possible), and then made the wise decision to evacuate. A call from our son saying they were safe gave us a sense of relief. It seemed an eternity before the news reporter announced that the storm had come on land wreaking havoc on the entire coast of Mississippi with Biloxi being hit hardest with over 200 mph winds.

The fear of lost lives was foremost on the minds of residents and those of us absorbing the horrors of the first reports of the devastation. The ring of the phone broke the silence as my husband reached for it hoping to hear our son's voice. It was Jimmy, and they had been given the okay to return to their home to assess, hopefully, few or minor damages.

Dining room after Katrina

When returning home, driving through Biloxi, it was difficult to comprehend the utter destruction that they were seeing. People looked for anything that resembled their home and even searched for family members and friends. Faces stained with tears, eyes gaunt, shoulders slumped, sitting where their home had been, with heads bowed on arms folded on drawn up knees. Block after block homes and businesses were leveled, landscaping was non-existent. Mighty oaks were toppled or stripped clean. Sadness exuded from not just humanity, but even inanimate objects.

Living room after Katrina

After reaching their home on the back bay, the outside structure appeared sound with not even a shingle off the roof. But stepping inside, it was a very different scene. A ten-foot surge of water from the back bay washed "in" and "out" again leaving a foot of mud and sludge throughout the first floor. Twelve-foot ceilings saved the second-floor bedrooms and his third-floor office. The image of a 3'x3' ottoman resting on top of the TV in the wall unit and the living room furniture scattered about topsy-turvy with no resemblance of the orderly arrangement 48 hours before were clear in our mind. The granite countertops were broken in half by the force of the water. The refrigerator was leaning on its side against the double oven, and the white wood rail on the staircase was splintered and hanging precariously in mid-air.

With heavy hearts, they realized how blessed they were. Their elderly neighbors were sitting on water-soaked sofas and chairs. The wife, who was not well, was sleeping on a portable beach lounge on their open deck. With no flood insurance, their outlook for rebuilding was bleak. Our teenage grandson with the help of some

 of his friends cleaned up the inside of their home.

Cleaning up after Katrina

A TV reporter showed lines of people waiting for small containers of water and ice from good Samaritans coming from many states to help in the crisis. The images of those waiting for the much-needed water and ice were planted deep in our minds.

Our son's family finally returned home. The next day, we loaded our motorhome with food, gallons of water and many large coolers of ice. My husband and our son-in-law pulled a trailer behind the motorhome loaded with grills, charcoal, folding tables and chairs, cooking utensils, etc. Our daughter drove a rented SUV also filled with supplies. My husband and son-in-law were prepared to cook outside for the neighbors.

I had stayed at home to prepare for the children if it was necessary for them to come here. With the schools closed, they loaded up the three youngest Destiny 10, Levi 9 and Devon 8 with their clothes and a few choice possessions and drove back to North Carolina in the rented SUV.

Kyle, their eighteen-year-old brother, stayed in Biloxi to help dad and mom. He had been our first and only grandchild for eight years. Remembering him as a three-year-old with red curls, I took him to Disney World every Saturday to see the Ninja Turtles. After the show, he would run with his autograph book wiggling his way through the crowd to get their autograph. I got as close as possible trying to see his red curls or his yellow high-top Converse tennis shoes to keep up with him.

As a teenager, he had begun playing roller and ice hockey. Grandpa and I followed him to every tournament whether it was in Biloxi, Disney World or St. Louis, Missouri. As the Captain of his roller hockey team, the Sea Hawks, they took home the First Place Trophy at the Junior Olympics in St. Louis.

He was invited to try out for the Canadian Maple Leafs' Ice Hockey Team. It was a great experience even though it didn't work out. As an adult, he worked with his dad building U.S. Embassies and Consulates in India, Mexico, Latvia, and Norway.

Leaving the motorhome parked in the driveway of their home, Jimmy and Lori lived in it while repairing the house. The walls had to be torn down to and including the wood studs. Kyle slept in his room on the second floor with no electricity or running water in extreme heat.

The three younger children spent the summer with us. We

Levi, Devon, Destiny, living in N.C.

had just taken them home to start school a few weeks before the storm. It was a blessing that we were not strangers to them. Many of their friends were sent to live with relatives they had never met before.

The children were in good spirits considering they had just left mom and dad in an unsettling situation. The boys shared a bedroom upstairs near our room. Destiny had the bedroom and bath downstairs.

She was ready to start school and focus on more than the recent destruction. However, I am sure the boys would have liked a little more vacation time. Nevertheless, Destiny and I went to South Macon Elementary School and met the principal, Mr. Bowles. He was very kind and reassuring to her. She felt very comfortable and said she thought it would be a good year. Their school records had been destroyed in Biloxi, but I was able to give Mr. Bowles adequate information for placement at the correct grade level. Mr. Bowles had said, to me, that since they were homeless, they would get consideration on lunch prices. Later, Destiny told me that she had no idea that

Levi, Devon and Destiny

they were considered homeless, but she took that in stride.

The teachers and staff had a positive influence on them. All three adjusted quickly and began to participate in school activities and field trips. I became involved in their educational process. Homework came after an afternoon snack and before play. Levi, being used to summer fun in North Carolina thought it would be the same. He commented that he didn't know it was going to be like that, but he learned it wasn't too bad. We feel they got a quality education while in the Macon County Schools. They got opportunities and awards that they would never have gotten in Biloxi.

They went home at the end of the school year. The house was livable, but construction was still going on. They had a family meeting talking about the situation, and the children chose to come back to North Carolina for the second school year.

Wanting the children to have a balanced life of fun and education, we enrolled Levi and Devon in Cub Scouts. We also took the boys and Destiny to the Skating Rink on Friday nights.

Getting them involved in church and church activities allowed them to have some incredible experiences with the youth group. Destiny and Levi went on several trips and got to hear some fantastic Christian speakers. Being able to go to these youth rallies and see several thousand other young people learning about what it means to live a Christian life gave them a strong start for living a Christ-filled life. All three children accepted Jesus as their savior while they were here. They were always at Pioneer Club on

Kyle, Destiny, Levi, Jimmy, Devon

Wednesday nights, attended Bible School, and participated in everything including performing in any activity.

Being too young to go with Destiny and Levi, on youth rallies, left a hole in Devon's heart when they were gone for a week. But Devon was an awesome skateboarder. So grandpa, Aunt Karyl, and I spent the week with Devon going to every skateboard park in western North Carolina. Later, when he returned to Biloxi, his skateboarding ability was recognized, and a local business owner sponsored him.

Grandpa could always come up with some way to entertain them and keep them busy. One project was to clear some of the Mountain Laurel bushes from the yard. He hooked a heavy chain to his old truck and fastened the other end around the plant. Making sure they were safe, he filled the cab with old cushions and let them pull up a bush when he yelled, "Go!" The pillows kept them from hitting their heads when the truck jerked forward. They thought they were driving and it was fun to them.

There was a trampoline, an electric Ferris Wheel that Grandpa had built when they were younger, and a trail around the property for a go-cart and dirt bikes. With all the privileges that these children had, things do not build bonds or develop positive attitudes or strong character. Good can come from any situation or circumstance if we look for it and embrace it.

I would like to share this from Destiny's perspective as a fifth-grader while attending South Macon Elementary School.

Her essay "Inspired by Hurricane Katrina" was entered in the Western Mountain Reading Council. She was a winner of the Macon County Young Authors writing contest and received a monetary gift of $20.00.

INSPIRED BY HURRICANE KATRINA

Hurricane Katrina was a devastating and deadly storm. It was the strongest recorded hurricane with winds over 200 mph. It was a Category 4 when it hit Biloxi, Mississippi, which is where my home is located. There was a tremendous storm surge of twenty-eight feet. About ten feet of water flooded the first floor of my house.

It changed my life in several good ways. I am very lucky that I still get to go to school. Some kids did not even start to school until October 3, 2005. I am also very fortunate that my grandparents had a home in North Carolina. One other good thing is that there will be a whole new look on the first floor of our house when it is finished.

The hurricane also affected my life in negative ways. I am going to school ten hours away from my parents and my older brother. My family only gets to visit occasionally. Most likely, I will not be able to see a couple of my friends because they have moved away. My parents have been living in my grandparents' motor home for over a month in our driveway in Biloxi. They have been cooking on a gas grill outside because they have no electricity.

It will take a long time to repair the first floor of our house since everything was destroyed. That means that I will be able to continue attending South Macon Elementary. I expect that things will turn out positively in the end. Katrina has made me realize how natural disasters affect people when it happens to them.

Destiny Kinsey
South Macon Elementary School
Grade 5
Western Mountains Reading Council

Congratulations! You're a winner in the Macon County Young Authors writing contest! Your writing will now go to the state contest, which is held in January. I will let you know the results of that as soon as they are reported. The Western Mountains Reading Council will be sending you a certificate or some form of recognition for your hard work.

You touched our hearts and brightened our day with your inspiring words. Dr. Porter and other members of the reading council who judged the contest asked me to tell you how much they enjoyed reading your stories and poems and how much they appreciate your participation. I hope you will share your writing with friends and family members, especially those who were the subject of your work.

I am so proud of you!
Mrs. Baker

Chapter Forty-Seven
Great-Grandchildren

When our grandson, Kyle Iroc, married, he and his wife blessed us with our first great-grandson, Landin Iroc in 2008. Three years later, our great-granddaughter, Aubriegh Marie arrived.

Landin has an understanding beyond his years. As a six-year-old, his ambition was to be a paleontologist and do research on dinosaurs. On one occasion, planning a project with grandpa, Landin reminded him they had to make a "schematic" before they could begin.

He and Aubriegh lived next door to us for several years. Aubriegh has an extraordinary humorous side, but when grandpa requires medical attention, even a simple band-aid, she immediately becomes serious and attentive to him.

They moved to Biloxi, Mississippi, but we have been privileged to have them visit us in North Carolina during the holidays, school breaks, and in the summers. They are a real pleasure to have any time as their mother has taught them to be respectful and appreciative of even the smallest things. Please and thank you are second nature with both. We are very blessed to have them in our life.

It wasn't until 2014 that Levi and his wife blessed us with Brentley Preston. Preston is a family name that followed four generations from great grandpa, James Preston, to grandpa, James Preston II, to dad, Levi Preston and has been used for generations in the Hampton and Kinsey lineage dating back to the 1800s.

Three-year-old Brently resembles his father when his father was a boy. He can tell us where to find anything that we may be searching for because he has already scouted out every nook and cranny in the house.

Brently's sister, Lexi Rose, our second great-granddaughter was next to warm our hearts and our home in 2017.

Destiny Brooke Lynn and her husband graced our lives with River Alexander and Rowan Antony in 2015 and 2016 respectively. Love and laughter are sure to entertain as River is a like a mighty rushing current moving rapidly, encouraging baby brother, Rowan to follow in the fray. Though they live in another state, we are blessed to have them visit us in North Carolina several times a year.

Kyle's next addition to the Kinsey clan is great-grandson, Diesel Kyle, in 2017. We can see he is growing into another special little boy by his pictures.

Larissa Inez Johnson, a special girl in my life, is my great, great niece. She and I share our love for theatre. She is performing with the Athens Little Theatre in Athens, Georgia.

God has blessed me with "extra years" to enjoy each of these children.

Landin Iroc Kinsey

Aubriegh Marie Kinsey

Brentley Preston Kinsey

River Alexander Lopez

Rowan Antony Lopez

Lexi Rose Kinsey

Deisel Kyle Kinsey

Larissa Inez Johnson

Chapter Forty-Eight
Brother's Funeral

In 2005 my brother, Harold died when our three grandchildren were living with us after Hurricane Katrina had destroyed the first floor of their home in Biloxi, Mississippi. Destiny ten, Levi nine, and Devon eight had never been to a funeral. I wasn't sure how it would affect them. I explained to them what it would be like, so they would know what to expect.

We left North Carolina early the next day and drove the four hours to the funeral home in Monroe, Georgia. When we arrived, we went into the viewing room for the last viewing before the service. The room was overflowing with family and friends. I took the children over to see Aunt Ruth, Harold's wife, sitting in her wheelchair, to give her hugs. Then, I took them over to the casket to see Uncle Harold, Levi took a quick look and immediately edged his way out through the crowd to get outside where he stayed until time for the service. Destiny and Devon walked over to the casket and were quite comfortable there and were in awe of the large diamond tie pin on his tie. Their eyes were fixed on it, and they came quietly over to ask if they could touch it. When I told them, "No, that would not be appropriate," they didn't say any more about it, but, the rest of the time, they planted themselves next to the casket and stood there like guards at Buckingham Palace.

Now, it was time for the service to begin and all three sat quiet and solemn. I noticed that Devon kept looking at me and finally he asked, "When are you going to cry?" I whispered to him that I was very sad, but Uncle Harold was in a better place, and he was okay. That seemed to satisfy him for the moment.

At the end of the service, as the pallbearers were rolling the coffin out, down the aisle, Devon swung his head with his eyes following the casket and said, in a slow southern drawl, "There goes your brother." It turned a serious moment into a little humor. Uncle Harold would have thought that was funny, too.

Chapter Forty-Nine
Rose Bowl Parade

Visiting our daughter and her husband the Christmas of 2013 in San Diego, California, they surprised us with a trip of a lifetime in an RV. The first night, we stayed in a park near Disney Land and were able to enjoy the fireworks that evening from the RV lot.

Driving several hours, the next day, we drove to Pasadena and located the parking space that our daughter, had pre-rented in the parking lot of the Volvo Dealership on the parade route.

She had also purchased tickets for us to go to the Float Decorating area to see the floats being built and decorated for the parade. These floats had been planned for months, but we were able to see them being decorated with millions of fresh flowers and foliage. They were designed like animals, buildings, cartoons and an array of other subjects. The colossal sizes were amazing.

Getting back to our parking space at the Volvo Dealership, we joined the hundreds of people putting out chairs on the sidewalk in the early evening to watch all the activity around us. The next morning, we could move our chairs into the street near a designated line to wait for the parade. Did I mention that we were traveling with four dogs? They were enjoying all the activity with us. Actually, they were excellent and stayed wherever Joe put their beds and food and water.

The night, before the parade, it was a party atmosphere! Few people went to bed as the parade of cars rolled through the streets beeping horns and waving banners. Onlookers were mesmerized by the silly string and wet marshmallows being thrown at the vehicles.

It obviously was fun for the people in the cars to see who could get their vehicle covered the most as they kept coming around again and again.

The next day was a beautiful sunny day for the spectacular parade with millions of fresh flowers in every conceivable design.

The following day we drove several hours through beautiful mountains to Semi Valley to visit President Ronald Reagan's Library. His grave on the hill facing the distant mountains was a sobering moment for me.

Air Force One was on display inside, and we were privileged to walk through it. It gave me a feeling of awe.

It was an exciting but humbling experience to sit at his desk, read from his teleprompter and see documents that I would never have been able to see otherwise. We took several days sightseeing on our way back to San Diego.

While there, we were blessed to be able to attend the Christmas Service at Dr. David Jeremiah's church in El Cajon, California. It was the amazing story of the birth of Christ with a live nativity that included every live animal. Even a camel walked down the aisle and took its place to complete the story. Listening to Dr. Jeremiah on television every week, Jim wanted to meet him in person, so against my thinking that he would not be available, Jim went over and talked to him. We attended another service the next week, and Dr. Jeremiah was very personable and remembered Jim and told him to be safe going back to North Carolina.

It was soon time for us to return to North Carolina. Thank you, Karyl and Joe, for an incredible Christmas experience!

Chapter Fifty
Changing the Landscape

Now that we were both retired, Jim was looking forward to enjoying the opportunity to choose his activities for the day. He no longer had the responsibility of managing employees for a large company with responsibilities that consumed his time at the store as well as when he was on vacation.

The one and a half-wood-ed acre that surround our house invited him with his creative mind to enjoy as many projects as he could imagine. And he did!

Deck

Building a large deck out back for entertaining along with a barbeque pit for cooking a whole pig has given us much pleasure. We have hosted three family reunions and have had a number of parties with friends.

Jim thought that perhaps a small pond with a waterfall would be a good substitute for the stream of rippling water that was not a natural part of our landscape.

Pond

Digging the hole for the pond with a pick and shovel in this hard, rocky ground was not factored in when he started digging. However, persistence prevailed, and the waterfall and small pool

181

were finally filled with water.

Listening to the water splash over rocks as it traveled down the waterfall and trickled into the pond gave me a reason to pull up a lounge chair under the shade of a tree at the edge of the pond, open a book and drift into another's life.

There was tranquility for a while until the three grandchildren visiting from Biloxi began squealing and jumping on the nearby trampoline. Coming back to my real life, I put my book down and enjoyed watching them bounce and turn flips. How dull life could be without children!

The electric Ferris Wheel now stood in the side yard with four individual swing seats painted the four primary colors as a reminder of earlier times with the grandchildren. Soon after I retired and moved to North Carolina, we started bringing
Destiny, five and Levi, four
up for the summer. When
Devon turned four, we in-
cluded him also. Many days
were busy watching them turning

Ferris Wheel

with the Ferris Wheel. One of us was always nearby, and Jim had installed seat belts for safety.

Anytime that we had people over, it wasn't just the children that enjoyed the Ferris Wheel; the adults tried it out too.

Before Zip Lines were popular, Jim had to try his hand at building one. Mentioning the idea to my brother-in-law, Sam, who was not enthused by the idea, Jim went ahead by himself to make it anyway. First, he attached a heavy cable to a huge oak tree with a circumfer-

Me on Zipline going up and down

ence of about four feet and ran it the 150' above the driveway stretching it up 50' to another oak. Considering the decline of the drive and the incline of the cable up to the other tree, after being pulled up to the top of the second tree, it should be a smooth ride back down to the starting point by the house.

On Jim's first try, he climbed up into the tree at its highest point and got into the chair for the ride. He had miscalculated the proper angle, and when he got about halfway down, the chair stopped. He was stranded dangling from the cable. Oh no, he had to call Sam and ask for help. With a big smile on his face, Sam came to the rescue.

After making the necessary adjustments, the zip line was ready for anyone who wanted to take a ride. The most fun was at Christmas when Kyle got a go-cart. We hooked a rope to the zip-line chair and go-cart. As Kyle drove down the driveway pulling the chair, it ascended to the highest point in the tree. Then he unhooked the rope from the go-cart, and the passenger rode back down.

When the big oak tree became diseased and had to be removed, it was like a best friend being put to rest.

The zip line was the favorite of Jim's amusement rides by most of those who rode it.

Each of Jim's projects changed the landscape around our home, and at eighty-four years of age, he still has plans for our seven great-grandchildren: Landin Iroc, Aubriegh Marie, Brentley Preston, River Alexander, Rowan Antony, Kyle Diesel and Lexi Rose along with my great-great niece, Larissa, to enjoy. He has a God-given talent for design and fun for the great-grandchildren now that the grandchildren have grown up.

Me on Zipline after coming down

Chapter Fifty-One

60th Wedding Anniversary

In 2014, for our 60th Wedding Anniversary, our daughter Karyl Scott and her husband, Joe, planned a 60th wedding anniversary celebration for us at The Boiler Room in Franklin, North Carolina. I

Group family photo

was excited, but I wondered if our son, Jimmy, would be able to be there since he lived and worked in Oslo, Norway. A few days before Christmas, he called and said that he would be here for both Christmas and the celebration.

I immediately started making plans for special foods and family traditions. The outside of the house had already been decorated with lights, and a manger scene greeted everyone who came onto the property. A sleigh in the shape of a rocket, loaded with Santa and a bag of gifts, hung over the driveway. Water sprayed from the back of the rocket to give the effect that it was just taking off to take happiness to children everywhere.

Every year that the children and grandchildren are here, we hang a stocking for each one with a small gift inside. That year, I hung fifteen stockings around the living room. Being together as a family is the greatest gift that I could ever receive.

When the special day for the Wedding Anniversary Celebration arrived, there were twenty-eight guests. Besides our children, Karyl and Jimmy, there were also our grandchildren, great-grandchildren and nieces and nephews. Some had traveled from nearby states.

The room was decorated with memorabilia and a collage of photographs from our lives for the past sixty years. My wedding dress was displayed at the entrance to

Jimmy, me, Jim and Karyl

the dining room. It was exciting to see family members, some getting

Me, Great-Niece Mia and Jim

reacquainted and everyone talking about things they remembered about the past.

After a wonderful dinner, everyone was milling around looking at the items on display and taking pictures when my great niece, Mia, walked in modeling my wedding dress. She looked stunning wearing the wedding dress I had worn sixty years before. It brought back tender memories.

Chapter Fifty-Two

Tree House

Dream, Fantasy or Reality?

For several years, the idea of building tree houses had become a phenomenon that was catching on from the West coast to the East

Tree House in Spring

coast. The concept not only reached North Carolina, but it specifically arrived in Otto.

Living in the mountains with trees of every size and multiple species, it seemed normal, to me, to see the possibility and the probability of constructing a tree house on our property.

Walking over three acres of the property looking for the perfect tree or trees to use, kept me focused on making this a reality. Jim finally joined me, fully convinced that I was serious.

Together, we chose a stately 110' tall oak with its gigantic limbs and magnificent character. Just 30' from the upstairs porch, it was conceivable that a bridge could connect the tree house to the porch.

Door designed as books

With the help of my son-in-law, three nephews, a grandson, and my husband's creative mind, the one-room tree house 16' x 14' was constructed using reclaimed wood and windows. Log siding

187

gave it the appearance of a log cabin. A genuine feeling emerged that I had a little house in the woods.

A 4' deck surrounds three sides of the tree house and wraps around the sturdy oak and allows room for outdoor furniture that encourages all who visit to enjoy the sights and sounds of God's creation from a bird's eye view of the surrounding Fish Hawk Mountains.

Mountain Laurel is abundant on the property, and it was designed around the deck for the handrails.

A writer's nook was the perfect place for me to write and be surrounded by books. The bookcases were handmade by my husband. Each one was constructed from small tree trunks that were cut into various lengths to accommodate shelves for every size book.

A special corner was set up with Children's books for our seven great-grandchildren and my great-great-niece, Larissa to enjoy.

Me, Jim, Landin and Aubriegh

Other books include novels of popular authors, Christian and Historical novels as well as books of local authors. There are also out of print and reference books.

My writing table is near a window that allows me to see the enormous tree trunk that helps support the tree house.

I designed the front door to resemble books of various colors arranged on bookshelves. Each book spine has a title of some of my performances with the Overlook Theatre and with a theatre group in Florida.

Just outside the front door hangs a special sign that welcomes everyone to "Grandma's Reading Tree."

The Tree House is no longer a dream nor a fantasy. It has become a reality!

Chapter Fifty-Three
Freedom
Why do we have freedom today?

Visualize with me those courageous men and women who left their homeland to achieve freedom for you and for me. Imagine the inner struggle they must have experienced in deciding whether to stay under British rule or to leave their family and friends to sail on a vast unknown ocean that would take them to a place where they could exercise freedom of speech and freedom of worship.

Feel the agony of the goodbyes as they stood for the last time on the rocky shore of their homeland. Sense the excitement and the anticipation of accepting the challenge of their search for a new home. The ship has anchored. The boarding deck is lowered. Hear the echo of footsteps on the wooden planks. See the smiles and tears as hands wave, one last time, to loved ones.

The loss of a husband or child has caused many to fear each day. Look into their eyes, see the despair of those asking themselves if they have made the right choice. Feel the pounding of the waves on the sides of the ship as it rocks furiously in the storm. Hear the muffled cries of the women and children. Now, it isn't an adventure, but it has become a dreaded event; one they cannot retreat from but must continue.

A triumphant day finally comes when they walk down that same gangplank onto their new homeland. It was a time for celebration even after all the heartaches they had endured. The tears, now, were tears of joy. Faces were radiant as their eyes surveyed the beauty of the coastline and the massive forests. Hope was renewed. Heartaches and fears were replaced with determination to fulfill the dreams of those lost. Those who had dreamed and planned for this day. They never gave up. They set examples for us and even lead our Founding Fathers to create a plan that we might have freedom today.

If we could just tell them how grateful we are for making our freedom, yours and mine, possible, that their sacrifices and hardships were not in vain. If they could only know, that this wonderful land is still free today.

Nothing is more important on the horizon today in our land. SPEAK UP! You have the liberty to do that. SPEAK OUT! LET FREEDOM REIGN!

Written and performed in the Senior
Follies by Mary Ann Kinsey

Chapter Fifty-Four

Family History

My great, great, great, great, great, great, grandfather, William Hampton came to America from Middlesex, England in the 1500s. I envision him as a strong and lean young man, but rather short as many of the Hampton men, today, are short. I believe he had a wife and came looking for opportunity. I also have confidence, that he felt a peace and contentment that he did not have back in England.

There was no more pressure to live under the king's demands. William was able to establish a home where he could teach his children the religious values that he believed. He found freedom of speech and religion in his new country and communicated that with those looking for freedom. It appears that others were anxious to sail to America, perhaps, on any ship or cargo boat that would accept them for a small fee. More Hamptons were waiting to come to America.

Settlers, likely, after a long day's work, would gather down by the water and gaze across the rolling waves waiting for the sight of a ship or cargo boat coming into the harbor bringing a family.

Wade Hampton I and Wade Hampton III arrived in the 1700 - 1800. Wade Hampton II came later. The Wade Hampton men being entrepreneurs, began constructing buildings that changed the outline of the towns. Roads were being built making travel easier and bringing towns closer together.

Many of the Hampton settlers were planters in South Carolina and Georgia with acres of land planted with cotton.

I visualize the bales of cotton being loaded onto wagons and being transported over rough, rocky wagon trails that gave the drivers a jolt every time those metal wheels jostled along. When a load reached the river, the cotton bales had to be loaded onto riverboats. As the boats chugged away from the dock and got into the river's strong current, they appeared to glide effortlessly over the water.

During the Civil War, better ways were needed for getting supplies to the troops as well as transporting commodities of the people. The battles that the soldiers were engaged in, most of them on foot, caused many injuries and casualties. That meant more doctors, nurses, and medical supplies were needed. Firearms, ammunition, uniforms, and food were an absolute necessity. Some of our foot soldiers fought during the winter snows without shoes.

The people began to talk about a better transport system. Then, the idea of a railroad crept into the conversations of the townspeople. As the idea grew, and the state of South Carolina needed land to build a railroad; some of the Hamptons began selling portions of their acreage to them for that purpose. It was a critical occupation during the Civil War.

The South Carolina Railroad went through the Hampton Plantation in Edgefield, South Carolina in 1833. James Hampton III, my Great, Great Grandfather saw the future of the railroad and sold his land to South Carolina in 1849 and worked for them as a fireman on the railway. It appears that he was a visionary with a business mind.

The South Carolina Railroad later became the Southern Railroad. My Great Grandfather, James Hampton worked for the railroad as an engineer. It was probably one of the most lucrative occupations at that time. It appears to have encouraged generations of Hamptons and their descendants to choose the railroad industry as their occupation.

Having large families was common. James Hampton, my Great Great Grandfather, had eight children. One of whom, was my Grandfather, Preston Brooks Hampton. He followed in his father's footsteps working for the railroad as a conductor and a railroad clerk before moving from South Carolina to Macon, Georgia. It was then he left his position with the railroad and went into the ministry. He followed his calling to preach God's word, leaving a job with a comfortable income to preach in a small church with a modest salary. He continued his ministry until his death in 1943. I am grateful for my Christian Heritage. Both of my grandfathers, Willis Tyler and Preston Brooks Hampton were ministers.

Augusta, Georgia, just twelve miles from the Hampton Plantation in Edgefield, South Carolina played an important part in the lives of the Hampton settlers just as the railroad affected their lives in 1933, the year that I was born. Augusta was an important trading center for eastern Georgia, northern and western South Carolina and a large section of North Carolina.

As I look back into my history and see how I emerged through the roots of my Family Tree, it is amazing to me, how family traits, similarities, and even occupations continued from generation to generation.

My older brother, Charles, was hired by the Central of Georgia Railroad in Macon as a teenager, to work in the railroad yard after our father was killed by a Central of Georgia Railroad Train. Having a good work ethic, and taking the responsibility of being the family provider for us, his brothers and sisters he slowly and eventually became a train engineer until he retired in the 1970's

Chapter Fifty-Five

Accomplishments and Awards

Accomplishments and Awards are nice to receive, but they reflect

Me- International Reading Conference Presenter

things that I was only able to accomplish with the support of those around me. None of us are self-sufficient in everything we do.

I was a member of Delta Kappa Gamma Society International, Seminole County Reading Council, Seminole County English Teacher's Council, Writing Team for Seminole County, Textbook Selection Committee for Seminole County Schools, Invitational Writing Institute at the University of Florida.

I received recognition for being a Presenter at both the Florida Reading Conference and the International Reading Conference along with my Team Teacher, for a program we designed and executed in our classes successfully.

I was awarded "Master Teacher" status by the Board of Educa-

Me and Mary S.

tion in the State of Florida, FACT Award - The Foundation Advance Community Through Schools, Disney's Teacherrific Award, Teacher of the Year for my school and runner-up for Seminole County Schools.

Lord, you establish peace for us;
All that we have accomplished you have
done for us.
Isaiah 26:12

Epilogue

Writing this book has been humbling, but a gratifying reflection of my life. Every person mentioned in this book was important to me along my journey, but there were hundreds more who touched my life.

As I stepped back in time, to my beginning and saw how God had brought me step by step to and through places that I could never have imagined, I am awed.

I was not always aware of God's control at each specific time in my life, but I see it clearly in retrospect.

My siblings get much of the credit for who I am today, but God gets all the credit for who I am.

I leave to my children, grandchildren, and great-grandchildren, for generations to come, the knowledge and hope that no matter where you begin in life, nor under what circumstances you find yourselves, you can fulfill your dreams and even surpass those dreams if you will put God first in your life and let Him direct your paths.

In all your ways
Acknowledge Him
And he will direct
Your paths.

Proverbs 3:5

Family Picture, 1968

Family Picture, 2017

Made in the USA
Lexington, KY
30 July 2018